Paul

An illustrated documentary

Paul is a crucial figure for understanding Christian belief. His writings form a major part of the New Testament, and his mission journeys took the Christian faith beyond the Jewish community to the world at large.

This lively and thorough account of his achievements follows the course of his life. Within that framework each of his letters is given extended analysis. Photographs, maps and charts help to bring the first century alive. Special articles on topics of more academic interest meet the syllabus requirements of the major GCE boards and other examinations.

With its awareness of current scholarship, faithfulness to historical detail and the New Testament text, and exciting presentation this book will be stimulating and informative for both the individual reader and schools and colleges.

Dr Drane has completed research on Paul at Manchester University, and taught R.E. at a comprehensive school. Married, with one son, he lectures in Religious Studies at the University of Stirling.

for Andrew

PAUL

John W. Drane

LION PUBLISHING

LION PUBLISHING
121 High Street, Berkhamsted, Herts

First edition 1976

ISBN 0 85468 043 6

Photographs on pages 23, 24 Museum of London; 63, 88, 93 American School of Classical Studies, Athens; 37 Camera Press; 65 The Mansell Collection; 66 Ecole Francaise d'Archéologie, Athens; 67 British Museum; 97 Maritime Museum, Haifa; 118 Clifford Shirley; the rest by David Alexander.

Printed in Great Britain by
Hazell Watson & Viney Ltd, Aylesbury, Bucks

Contents

Continued over

Chapter 5. Paul the Pastor

Chapter 6. Paul reaches Rome

Chapter 7. Paul in Prison

Chapter 8. 'A Man in Christ'

Illustrations

Paul's Life and Writings

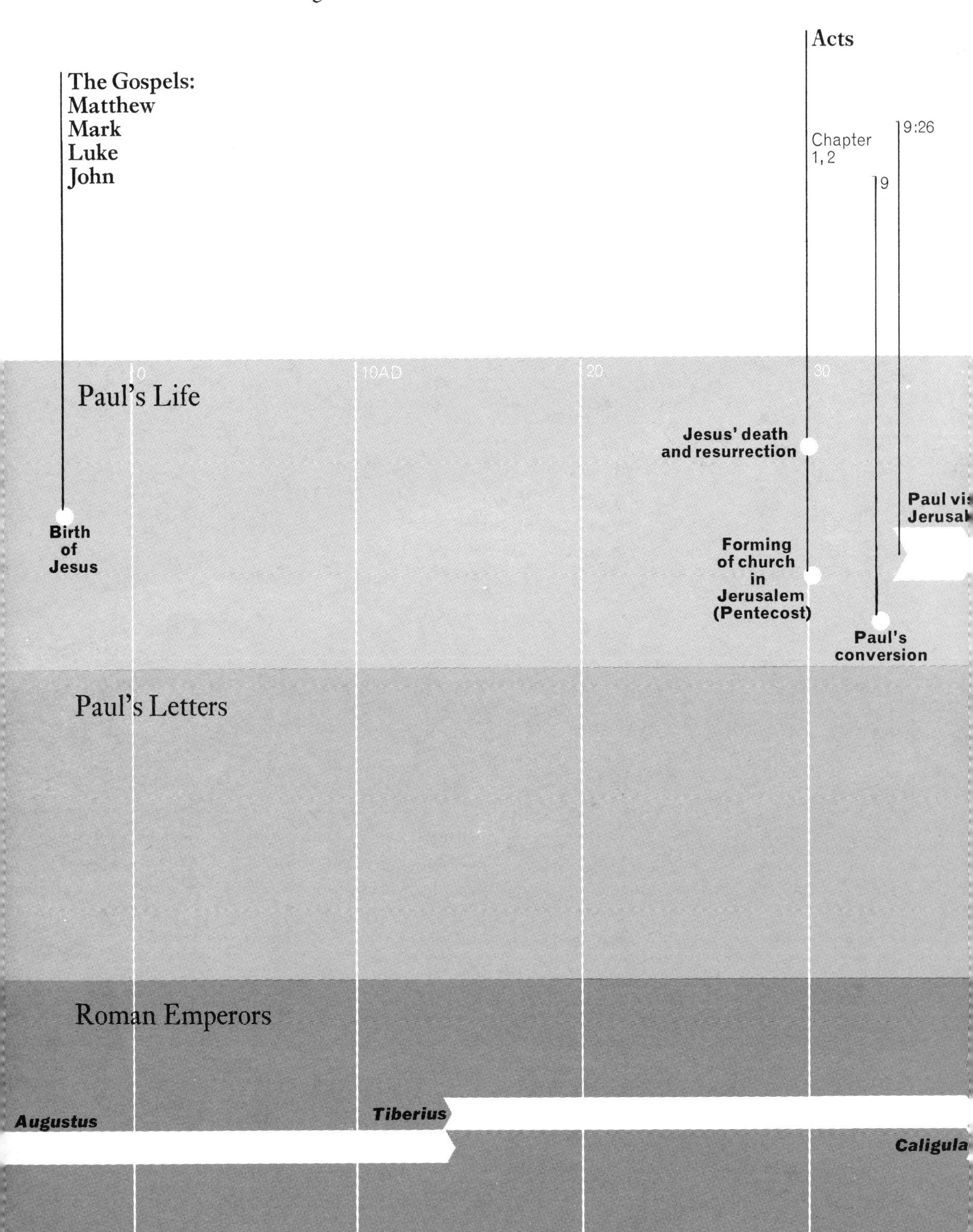

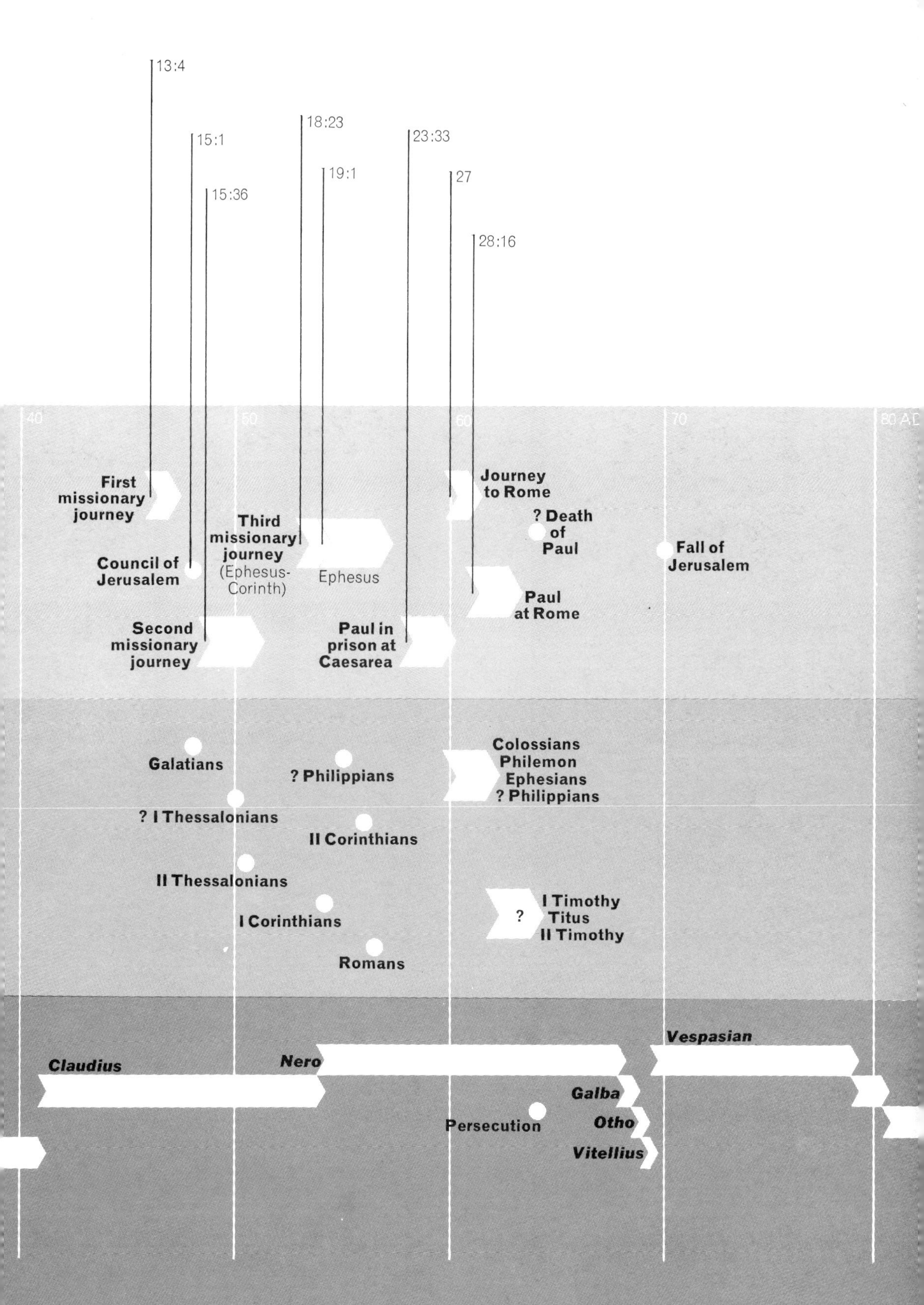
13:4
15:1
15:36
18:23
19:1
23:33
27
28:16
40
50
60
70
80 AD
First missionary journey
Council of Jerusalem
Second missionary journey
Third missionary journey (Ephesus-Corinth)
Ephesus
Paul in prison at Caesarea
Journey to Rome
? Death of Paul
Paul at Rome
Fall of Jerusalem
Galatians
? I Thessalonians
II Thessalonians
I Corinthians
? Philippians
II Corinthians
Romans
Colossians
Philemon
Ephesians
? Philippians
?
I Timothy
Titus
II Timothy
Claudius
Nero
Persecution
Galba
Otho
Vitellius
Vespasian

The World of the New Testament

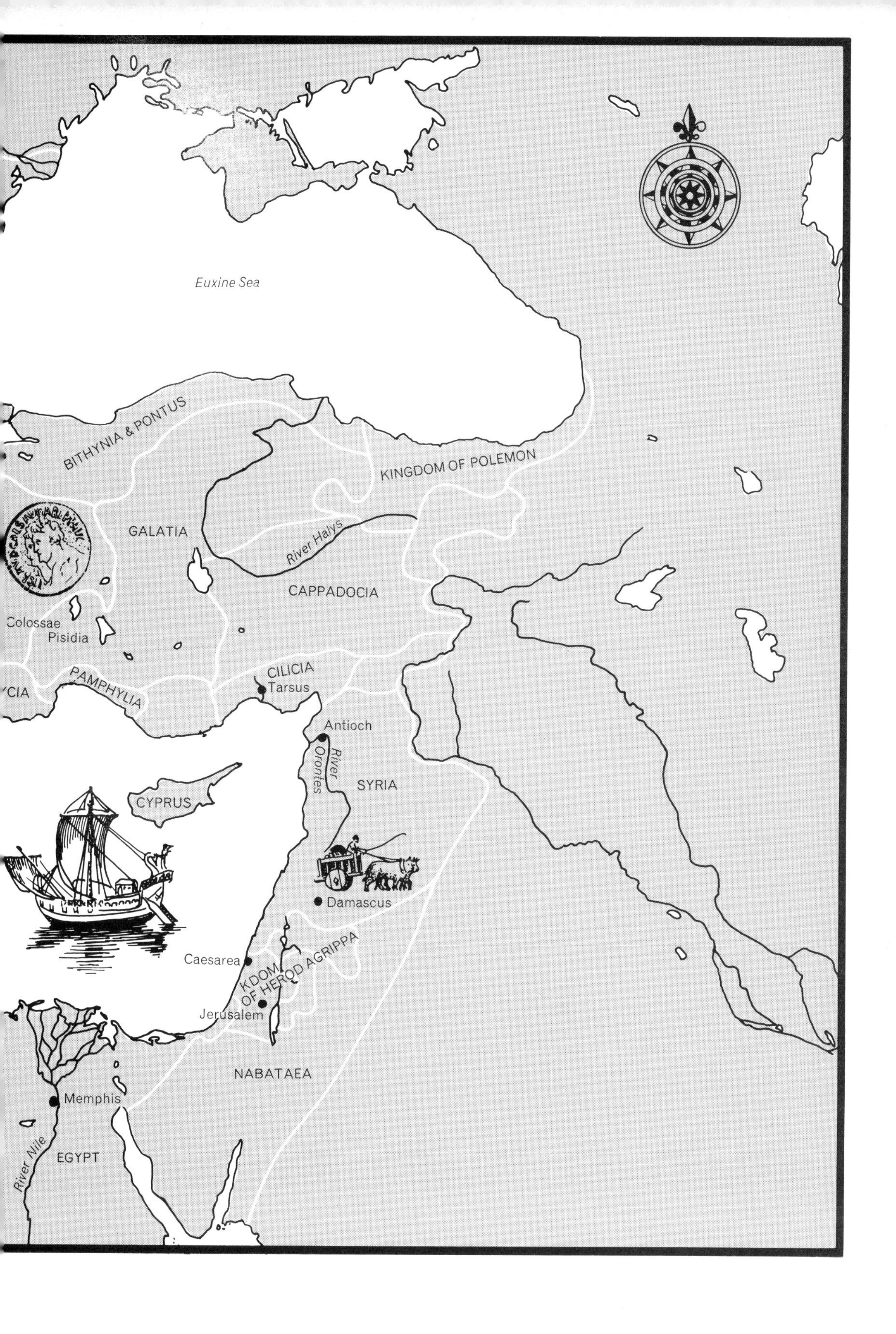

Euxine Sea
BITHYNIA & PONTUS
KINGDOM OF POLEMON
GALATIA
River Halys
CAPPADOCIA
Colossae
Pisidia
CILICIA
Tarsus
PAMPHYLIA
YCIA
Antioch
River Orontes
SYRIA
CYPRUS
Damascus
Caesarea
KDOM OF HEROD AGRIPPA
Jerusalem
NABATAEA
Memphis
EGYPT
River Nile

1 Who was Paul?

'A MAN small of stature, with a bald head and crooked legs, in a good state of body, with eyebrows meeting and nose somewhat hooked, full of friendliness; for now he appeared like a man, and now he had the face of an angel.' This was how Paul was described in a second-century apocryphal writing, *The Acts of Paul and Thecla*.

For the Jews of the Greek city of Thessalonica, Paul was the man who had 'turned the world upside down', and who was now trying to do the same thing with their synagogue.

Acts 17:6

A recent writer, Donald Guthrie, in his book *Galatians*, sees him as 'an ardent adherent of Judaism . . . essentially a preacher . . . no theoretical theologian', and 'an intensely human man' who had experienced everything he wrote about.

But let's begin at the beginning, and listen to the way Paul described himself:

'I am a Jew, born at Tarsus in the Roman province of Cilicia, a citizen of a very important city. My upbringing was thoroughly Jewish in every way. I was also particularly fortunate in being born into a family on which Roman citizenship had been conferred, and I am especially proud of this privilege. I was educated in the city of Jerusalem at the school of the famous teacher Gamaliel, according to the strictest interpretation of the Jewish Law as laid down by the Pharisees. I was so zealous for the traditions of my people that I soon advanced in my religious faith far beyond most of my contemporaries. I could even claim to be almost faultless in my obedience to the Old Testament Law.'

Acts 21:39; 22:3; 22:28; Galatians 1:13–14; Philippians 3:5–6

Paul as a child

There were probably two distinct periods in Paul's early life: his childhood, spent in Tarsus, and his youth and early manhood, spent in Jerusalem. The words translated 'brought up' in Acts 22:3 could indicate that Paul was only a baby when he moved from Tarsus to Jerusalem. But most scholars think they refer only to his education. Since he went back to Tarsus after he became a Christian, this seems the most obvious meaning of the expression.

Acts 9:30

First and foremost, Paul was a Jew, and proud of it. He was also proud of Tarsus, which was a university town and centre of government and trade. But he had no real affection for its culture, which was Greek and pagan. Paul's parents were good Jews, as well as being Roman citizens. Though they tried to shield him from the pagan influences of a city like Tarsus while he was a boy, it was the kind of place where any bright child would be bound to pick up some of the language and ideas of pagan Greek culture. The general influence of this kind of city is probably enough to explain the two references to Greek literature which we find in Paul's letters and sermons: a reference to the poet Epimenides, and to Aratus.

Acts 17:28
Titus 1:12

Paul's early life was spent in Tarsus. These Turkish school-children of modern Tarsus stand in front of one of the few structures remaining from Paul's time.

Paul the student

Quite early in life, Paul's parents decided that he should become a student and teacher of the Jewish Law. As a small child in Tarsus, he learned the traditions of the Jewish people through regular instruction at the local synagogue. His first Bible was probably the Greek edition of the Old Testament, the Septuagint. The Old Testament had been translated from the original Hebrew by Jewish scholars living in Alexandria in Egypt about 150 BC. We sometimes call it LXX, the Roman number 70, because of a tradition that there were seventy translators. Most Jews living outside Palestine used this Greek version of the Old Testament rather than the Hebrew Bible.

While he lived in Tarsus, Paul also learned the art of tent-making, for every student of the Jewish Law was expected to learn a practical trade as well as doing his studies. This was something that was of great value to Paul later in his life, for it enabled

him to earn his own living while he was engaged in his missionary work.

Paul was soon sent away from Tarsus to the centre of the Jewish world, Jerusalem. Here he became a student of the learned Rabbi (or teacher) Gamaliel, who was the grandson and successor of the great Rabbi Hillel (about 60 BC–AD 20). Hillel had taught a more advanced and liberal form of Judaism than his rival, Shammai. What Jesus said about divorce may have been provoked by the arguments of the followers of these two rabbis. Hillel declared that a man could divorce his wife if she displeased him in any way – even if she burned his dinner! But Shammai took the view that divorce was justified only in the event of some serious moral sin. What Paul himself later wrote on this subject shows that he must have changed his mind after he became a Christian.

Mark 10:1–12

See 1 Corinthians 7:10–11

Yet Paul did gain at least one great benefit from his education in the tradition of Hillel. Shammai had refused to see any place for the Gentiles (those people who were not Jews) in the purposes of God. His rival, however, had not only welcomed them, but positively set out to evangelize them. No doubt it was from Gamaliel that Paul first learned what a great job was waiting to be done among the non-Jewish people of the Roman Empire.

Paul progressed well in his studies at Jerusalem, and soon came to a position of prominence there. He became so important that when Christians were being tried for their faith, he was in a position to 'cast his vote' against them, either in a synagogue assembly or in the supreme council of the Jews, the Sanhedrin.

Acts 26:10

So much for what we know about Paul's background and education. We have sketched briefly the main outline of events almost up to the time when he became a Christian. Now we must dig beneath the surface, and see what we can discover in his early life that will help us to understand his complex personality and some of the darker corners of his letters.

Three main influences must have been at work on the young Paul's mind: Judaism, Greek philosophy and the Mystery Religions.

Paul and the Jews

Paul himself never mentions Greek or pagan influences, but he makes many statements about his Jewish background and upbringing. He makes a great deal of the fact that he was a good Pharisee. As we read the letters he wrote as a Christian, it is obvious that he still retained the best beliefs of his teachers. One of the main rivals of the Pharisees was a group called the Sadducees. The two groups represented, respectively, the liberal and the conservative wings of Judaism. At every point of dispute between the two groups, Paul takes up and often improves the Pharisees' viewpoint:

Opposite. Herod's Temple in Jerusalem was the focus of Jewish religious activity. In the outer area, the 'Court of the Gentiles' (on the left), was a thriving market in sacrificial animals; and in the porticos men would gather to listen to religious teachers. Inside the 'wall of partition', beyond which only Jews could pass, the daily pattern of worship and sacrifice was continued by priests and Temple servants.
In this reconstruction of Herod's Temple the details of decoration are mainly guesswork.

- Pharisees believed that history had a goal and a purpose. They held that God was ordering events according to his own plan, which would culminate in the coming of a Messiah to lead his people. This was something Paul could readily accept as a Christian. In Romans 9–11 he argues that God is ordering the course of history with a view to the ultimate incorporation of the Jews into the Christian fellowship. He is arguing like a good Pharisee – though at the same time he went further, for Paul knew that the Messiah had already come, in the person of Jesus Christ.
- Pharisees believed in a future life. Paul stressed this to his own advantage when on trial before the Sanhedrin, and again before Herod Agrippa II: 'I stand here on trial for hope in the promise made by God to our fathers . . . And for this hope I am accused by Jews, O king! Why is it thought incredible by any of you that God raises the dead?' But as a Christian Paul went further. He knew that no one could guarantee that there would be a resurrection apart from the fact that Jesus Christ had risen from the dead: 'Now if Christ is preached as raised from the dead, how can some of you say that there is no resurrection of the dead? . . . Christ has been raised from the dead, the first fruits of those who have fallen asleep. For as by a man came death, by a man has come also the resurrection of the dead.'

Acts 23:6–10

Acts 26:6–8

1 Corinthians 15:12, 20–21

● Pharisees believed in the existence of angels and demons. The Sadducees did not. Again, Paul retained this belief as a Christian, but transformed it in the light of his experience of Christ. On the cross, Christ had conquered the powers of evil. Because of this, Christians are 'more than conquerors through him who loved us'. No angel could ever rival the risen Lord whom Paul served, and in whom 'all the fullness of God was pleased to dwell'.

Romans 8:37

Colossians 1:19

It was not only in terms of belief that Paul continued to show his Jewish background. The very way he writes, using the Old Testament to 'prove' his theological points, is taken directly from his training as a Pharisee. No one who reads his letter to the Galatians can fail to be amazed, and sometimes amused, by the way Paul draws very unusual meanings from what to us are quite straightforward Old Testament passages. For instance, he argues like a Jewish rabbi when he claims that the promises made to Abraham referred to one single person, Jesus Christ, because the Greek word for 'offspring' (like its English equivalent!) is singular and not plural in form. Like the rabbis, Paul argues from single isolated texts, and can link up texts taken from completely different, and unrelated, parts of the Old Testament.

Galatians 3:16

Opposite page. A strict observer of Judaism in modern Israel. The box tied to his forehead is called a phylactery, and contains passages from the Jewish Law (see Deuteronomy 6:8).

An orthodox Jew reads the Law (or *Torah*) at the Wailing Wall in modern Jerusalem. Some of the stones in the Wall formed part of the structure of Herod's Temple.

The synagogue was of great importance in Jewish life. It formed the centre of worship, education and government of the civil life of the local Jewish community. This reconstruction of a synagogue of Paul's time shows the Scriptures in a prominent position, symbolizing their importance for the Jews.

Yet there was one crucial point at which Paul departed from his Jewish heritage. The Pharisees were legalists. They insisted on a detailed observance not only of the written Law of the Old Testament, but of traditional laws and customs for which there was no biblical authority. What is more, they claimed that if a man did not observe all of these in every particular, he could never attain to full salvation. Paul had been driven to the depths of despair as he vainly tried to be a good Pharisee and keep all the Law. He knew he could never do it. Therefore he could never truly know God. In an optimistic moment he once said that 'as to righteousness under the Law' he was 'blameless'. But at heart he knew that there was a greater power than his own at work to prevent him from ever keeping the whole Law. Even the success he did manage to achieve was far from adequate: 'I am carnal, sold under sin. I do not understand my own actions. For I do not do what I want, but I do the very thing I hate.' The more Paul tried to do good, the more impossible he found it.

Philippians 3:6

Romans 7:14–15

It was only because he was such a faithful Pharisee that he was able to appreciate the importance of what God had done for humans in Jesus Christ. Pharisaism was a mirror in which Paul saw his own shortcomings so clearly revealed that he seemed to be 'the foremost of sinners'. But in Jesus Christ he saw a reflection of what he could become by the free grace of God: 'God has done what the law . . . could not do: sending his own Son in the likeness of sinful flesh and for sin, he condemned sin in the flesh . . . So then . . . if by the Spirit you put to death the deeds of the body you will live . . . the Spirit helps us in our weakness.'

1 Timothy 1:15

Romans 8:3, 12, 13, 26

Paul and the philosophers

Of the many philosophical schools of the time, **Stoicism** was probably the most congenial to Paul. This was a philosophy which identified God with the 'Reason' found throughout the universe. Stoicism was most influential in its ethical teaching about the duty and the unity of mankind. Conscience showed a man what was good, and it was up to him resolutely to set his will to do his duty. One or two of the great Stoics came from Tarsus, and Paul may have remembered something about their teachings from his youth.

Some scholars have suggested that Paul's acquaintance with Stoic philosophy was closer than this. In 1910 Rudolf Bultmann, the great German New Testament scholar, pointed out that Paul's reasoning sometimes resembles the Stoics' arguments. Both use rhetorical questions, short disconnected statements, an imaginary opponent to raise questions, and frequent illustrations drawn from athletics, building, and life in general. It is even possible to find phrases in Paul's teaching which could be taken to support Stoic doctrine; for example the statement that 'all things were created through him and for him. He is before all things, and in him all things hold together'. No doubt Paul would know and sympathize with many Stoic ideals. But there are outstanding and quite fundamental differences between Paul's Christianity and Stoicism:

Colossians 1:16–17

- Stoicism was based on philosophical speculations about the nature of the world and of man. Its real 'god' was abstract human reason. Christianity is quite different. It is based firmly on the historical facts of the life, death and resurrection of Jesus Christ.

See 1 Corinthians 15:3–11

- The Stoic 'god' was an ill-defined abstraction, sometimes associated with the whole universe, sometimes with Reason, and sometimes even with the element of fire: 'What god we know not, yet a god there dwells.' Paul's God, on the other hand, was a personal Being revealed in Christ: 'In him all the fullness of God was pleased to dwell.'

Seneca, *Letters* 41.2, quoting Virgil

Colossians 1:19

- The Stoic found 'salvation' in self-sufficiency. He sought to win mastery of himself so that he could live in harmony with nature. 'The end of life is to act in conformity with nature, that is, at once with the nature which is in us and with the nature of the universe . . . Thus the life according to nature is that virtuous and blessed flow of existence, which is enjoyed only by one who always acts so as to maintain the harmony between the daemon within the individual and the will of the Power that orders the

Diogenes Laertius vii.1.53

universe.' For Paul salvation was completely different from this. He found it not in dependence on himself, but in submission to Jesus Christ: 'I have been crucified with Christ; it is no longer I who live, but Christ who lives in me; and the life I now live in the flesh I live by faith in the Son of God, who loved me and gave himself for me.'

Galatians 2:20

● Stoicism had no future: it was a religion of hopelessness. The majority of men were considered incapable of reaching any moral maturity. They were destined to be destroyed as one cycle of the world's history followed another, only to be reborn, or reincarnated, again so that the whole cycle could be repeated. But Christianity contrasted with this, asserting that the world as we know it would end decisively with the future personal intervention of Christ himself. Then a completely new world order would emerge.

See 1 Corinthians 15:20–28

The influence of the Stoics on Paul must be reckoned to be minimal. None of us can escape using words and phrases, even religious ones, with which we are familiar in other contexts. But if Paul ever used the language of the Stoics, he gave it a new meaning. For his own message of salvation through Christ was a long way from the Stoic message of salvation through self-discipline.

Paul and the Mystery Religions

Throughout the Roman Empire in the first century there were a number of strange cults, commonly known as the Mystery Religions. These combined ideas from eastern religions, such as Zoroastrianism or Judaism, with ideas from the religious traditions of Egypt, Greece, and Rome. Their great attraction was that they offered an emotional satisfaction to people who had discarded the gods of ancient Greece and Rome as mere superstitions, but who found Stoicism and the other philosophies dull and beyond their mental grasp. One of these religions later came to be closely associated with Christianity. It was given the name 'Gnosticism', because it claimed to show the way to a secret 'knowledge' (*gnōsis* in Greek), the possession of which was a man's only hope of salvation.

There are several superficial resemblances between the Mystery Religions and the Christian faith. Both came to Rome from the east. Both offered 'salvation' to their followers. Both used initiation rites (Christian baptism) and a sacramental meal (the Christian communion). Both referred to their saviour god as 'lord'. The two often became intertwined as converts from the Mysteries entered the church, sometimes bringing their Mystery beliefs with them. It was probably an event like this that was the cause of much of the trouble in the church at Corinth, about which Paul wrote in his letters to the Corinthians (see also chapter 5).

Because of these resemblances between Christianity and the Mysteries, some scholars have thought that what Paul did was

Below. Paul may occasionally have borrowed words from the Greek philosophers; but his own message was fundamentally different. This head of a philosopher dates from the second century AD and was discovered at Ephesus.

Mithraism was the most powerful Mystery Religion in the Roman Empire in Paul's time. Worshippers believed that the god Mithras would save the faithful and help them reach heaven. Here Mithras, a Persian god, is killing the bull as a sacrifice.

to change the simple ethical teaching of Jesus into a kind of Mystery Religion. No one today holds this view. There is no real historical evidence to support it. What evidence there is tends to show quite the opposite:

- The Mysteries were always ready, and even eager, to combine with other religions. This was something that Christians always rejected, believing that they alone had the full truth revealed to them by Christ.
- Much of the evidence that was claimed to show that Paul was a Mystery adherent is now seen to be false. For instance, the title 'lord' applied to Jesus is now known to come not from Mystery Religions, but from the Old Testament. The Christian confession of faith 'may our Lord come' (recorded in its Aramaic form, *Marana-tha*) shows that the very earliest church in Jerusalem, the only one to speak Aramaic, must have given Jesus that title long before Paul came on the scene.

  1 Corinthians 16:22
- What impressed the pagan world was not the similarity of Christianity to other religions, but its difference from them. The accusation most often made against Christians was of atheism, because they would not admit even the possibility that other gods could exist.

No doubt Paul knew of the Mystery Religions and their resemblances to Christianity. They told of gods coming down in the form of men; of salvation as 'dying' to the old life; of a god giving immortal life; and of the saviour god being called 'lord'. It is possible that Paul, who was ready to be 'all things to all men',

1 Corinthians 9:22

The religion of Mithras was tough. It involved tests like being walled up for several days, and appealed particularly to soldiers. However women were not allowed to participate, and its limited appeal weakened its resistance to Christianity. This little temple of Mithras was discovered at Walbrook, London.

sometimes deliberately used their language. But it is more likely that he used it unconsciously. For educated people in his day would use the language of the Mystery Religions as easily and as uncommitedly as we often use the language of popular astrology today. Paul shows no detailed knowledge of the Mystery Religions. He makes no clear reference to any of their ceremonies. In spite of this many modern scholars think an early form of Gnosticism, rather than the Mystery Religions in general, exercised a powerful influence on the church in the first century. We will look at some of their claims when we deal with Paul's letters to the church at Corinth (see chapter 5).

Paul's background included three worlds of thought: the Jewish, the Greek and the Mystery. Each one of these can shed a certain amount of light on his personality and his teaching. But we would be foolish to regard Paul as merely the natural product of his cultural surroundings. He regarded himself supremely as 'a man in Christ'. Whatever he may have gained from these other sources, he recognized in his new Lord a power greater than them all, and someone for whom he counted everything else as 'refuse'.

2 Corinthians 12:2

Philippians 3:8

2 Paul the Persecutor

One of the most cherished beliefs of the Jews, and one that Paul no doubt shared, was that God would soon intervene in history to rescue his chosen people Israel from the domination of alien political forces. They believed that God would set them up as one of the great nations of the world by the arrival of the 'Messiah' or 'Christ'. Both words mean 'anointed one': 'Messiah' is Hebrew, and 'Christ' is Greek. He would arrive in dramatic fashion, a royal figure of the ancient house of David. He would march on Jerusalem with his followers, enter the Temple and drive the hated Romans from the land.

So when Jesus of Nazareth appeared evidently claiming to be the Messiah, it was not surprising that the Jews did not recognize him as the kind of deliverer they were looking for. Far from being royal his birth took place in obscurity. He had no army, and often spoke in terms that showed his contempt for physical violence. When he entered the Temple in fulfilment of the prophecy of Zechariah, it heralded not victory over the Romans but humiliation and death at their hands.

Luke 1 and 2; John 1:46
Matthew 5:38–42
Mark 11: 1–19; Zechariah 9:9

Paul shared the contempt felt by the Jewish leaders for this crucified 'Messiah'. He despised even more the activities of the followers of this pseudo-Christ. For they were claiming that after his degrading execution he had risen from the dead, and that God had recognized him as the true Messiah by giving him a place of high honour.

Acts 2:22–24

Now Paul could conceivably have had some respect for Jesus himself. After all, he had been an ethical teacher, and said many things with which the Jewish rabbis could agree. But his followers had nothing to commend them at all. They were ignorant, uneducated men. What right had they to tell the religious leaders of the day that they had been mistaken, that they had demanded the death of none other than God's own Son?

Acts 4:13

Persecution

When one of Jesus' followers, a man called Stephen, dared to say in public that the days of the Jewish religion and its Temple were finished, Paul and his fellow-Pharisees knew that the time had come for action. No longer was it enough to regard these followers of 'the Way', as they called themselves, as amiable cranks. They posed a dangerous threat to the Jewish religious system.

Acts 7:2–53

So Stephen was stoned to death by a Jerusalem mob. Paul himself stood by, happy to guard the coats of the executioners while they did their evil work.

Acts 7:54–8:1

But Paul was more than just a coat-minder. He was a crafty man, and an influential Pharisee. When he saw that the Christians were beginning to move out of Jerusalem to other places, he realized that, far from having solved the problem, the way the Jews were persecuting Stephen and the others was only helping the Christian cause to spread to other parts of the Roman Empire.

One of the places where these fanatics were congregating was Damascus, an independent city within the Nabatean kingdom.

At the time Aretas IV (9 BC–AD 40) ruled over the Nabatean kingdom, though he had no direct authority over Damascus itself. This was not the first time that Damascus had served as a haven for religious refugees from Judea. According to the *Zadokite Fragments* (documents which stem from a Jewish sect associated with the people who wrote the Dead Sea Scrolls) a large number of Jews had fled there just before 130 BC. Since these people had been able to live independently of the authorities in Jerusalem, no doubt the early Christians thought they could do the same. In addition, the Jewish communities formed by these earlier immigrants would provide an ideal audience to which to proclaim the message of Jesus as Messiah.

2 Corinthians 11:32–33

But the Christians had reckoned without Paul. He remembered that earlier in his nation's history the Romans had given to the high priest in Jerusalem the right to have Jewish criminals extradited from other parts of the empire. So he went to the high priest to ask for a letter authorizing him to pursue the Christians to Damascus, and bring them back to Jerusalem for trial and sentence. It was while doing so that Paul had a remarkable experience which was to alter the course of his whole life.

1 Maccabees 15:15–24

Acts 9:1–2

Paul meets Jesus

This experience is described in detail in three different places in the book of the Acts, which shows just how important it was not only in Paul's life, but in the entire history of the early church. In Acts 9:3–19 we have Luke's summary account of what happened; in 22:6–16 we have a personal account given by Paul when defending himself before a Jewish mob in Jerusalem; and in 26:9–23 we have another account given by Paul, this time in his defence before Herod Agrippa II.

The three accounts build up a composite picture rather than agreeing precisely in every detail. Two of them were from Paul himself; the other is Luke's own summary of what happened. Luke was simply recounting the broad outline of what took place; Paul on each occasion had particular reasons for expressing himself as he did.

The different accounts of Paul's conversion

There are three main differences in points of detail in the accounts of Paul's conversion.

- In Acts 9:7 Paul's companions heard the voice of the risen Christ, but saw no *person*. They may have seen the bright light. In 22:9 Paul says they 'saw the light but did not hear the voice of the one who was speaking to me'. What they heard was presumably a sound, but not an intelligible voice. The account in chapter 26 does not refer to the companions either seeing or hearing.
- In Acts 9:4 and 22:7 the only person mentioned as falling to the ground is Paul, the central figure in the drama. But this need not exclude the possibility that the others fell to the ground, as in 26:14.
- In Acts 9:6 and 22:10 Paul is told to go on to Damascus, where he will be told what to do. In 26:16 his commission to be an apostle is given at the time of the

Stephen was stoned after attempting to defend himself against the charge of blasphemy in a Jewish court. The execution may have taken place outside St Stephen's Gate, Jerusalem, viewed here from the Mount of Olives.

vision. Possibly Paul did not wish to bore Agrippa with the details of his story, and so compressed it into this form.

These distinctions are not of great importance, and can easily be explained by the different purpose of the narrative in each case. Indeed the fact that these variations in emphasis have been preserved by Luke gives us greater confidence in him as a credible historian. If he had invented the story, he would have been more likely to have made sure that each account of it was identical with the others in form and language.

In all essential points, the three accounts are agreed. Paul was travelling along the road to Damascus, bent on wiping out the Christians there, when 'a light from heaven, brighter than the sun' shone down on him, and he was challenged by the voice of the risen Christ, 'Why do you persecute me?'

Acts 26:13

Acts 9:4; 22:7; 26:14

Paul was a changed man. In that instant he realized that the hopes he had entertained as a Jew were false. The divine Messiah had come not as a soldier but as a servant; the battle he fought and won was not against the Romans but, as Paul expressed it later, against the 'principalities and powers'. Jesus of Nazareth, whom Paul had so despised, was standing before him as the Son of God and Lord of all, demanding that he should recognize Christ's rule over his nation, and over Paul's own life. Paul responded by accepting the demands of the risen Christ. As he later told Agrippa in simple yet telling words: 'I was not disobedient to the heavenly vision.'

Ephesians 6:12

Acts 26:19

Paul, who had hated the Christian faith, was to become its greatest advocate. Though he might have boasted about his great achievements in Judaism, from now on his life was totally dominated by the risen Christ who appeared to him on the Damascus road, and revolutionized his life and thinking.

Paul gives several accounts of the decisive events on the Damascus Road, when the risen Christ spoke to him. The encounter meant a radical change in Paul's life.

After this shattering encounter, Paul continued to Damascus,

When he arrived at Damascus, Paul lodged with a man named Judas who lived in Straight Street, which is today a busy shop-lined road. A Roman gateway and parts of the city walls of Paul's time still stand in modern Damascus.

physically blinded by the bright light, but with the eyes of his mind now opened by the one he had been persecuting. He was so overwhelmed by his experience that when he arrived at his lodgings in Damascus, he was unable to eat or drink for three days.

Acts 9:9

Paul at Damascus

Acts 9:10–19; 22:12–16

God's plan for Paul's life covered the details, as well as the broad outline. The risen Christ sent Ananias, a Christian living in Damascus, to visit Paul with a special message and the power to restore his sight. Paul was now baptized and spent some time with the Christians in Damascus. As he met with them Paul must have realized for the first time that in Christian fellowship he could be united with men and women who on any other ground would have been abhorrent to him. When he wrote later to the churches of Galatia, he emphasized the fact that faith in Christ should produce reconciliation amongst men. But he could write

Galatians 3:28–29

in this way only because he had experienced it in his own life. The ignorant and uneducated people whom he had determined to hound to death now became his closest friends.

But Paul did not forget his original purpose in coming to Damascus, which was to visit the Jewish synagogues of the city. He went straight to the Jews, who were no doubt expecting his arrival. But his message was most unexpected. Instead of denouncing the Christian faith he proclaimed it, and made known his new allegiance to Jesus the Messiah.

Acts 9:20–25

In Galatians 1:17 Paul mentions a brief visit to a place called 'Arabia' (probably an area near Damascus) before returning to Damascus for three years. This is not inconsistent with Acts, where it is stated that he remained in Damascus for 'many days'. He may have gone to 'Arabia' immediately after meeting Ananias, or he may have gone there after some initial preaching in the Jewish synagogues.

Acts 9:23

Eventually, Paul found it impossible to stay any longer in the city of Damascus. Both the Jews and the city authorities were eager to get rid of him, so his friends secretly let him down over the city wall in a basket.

2 Corinthians 11:32
Acts 9:23–25

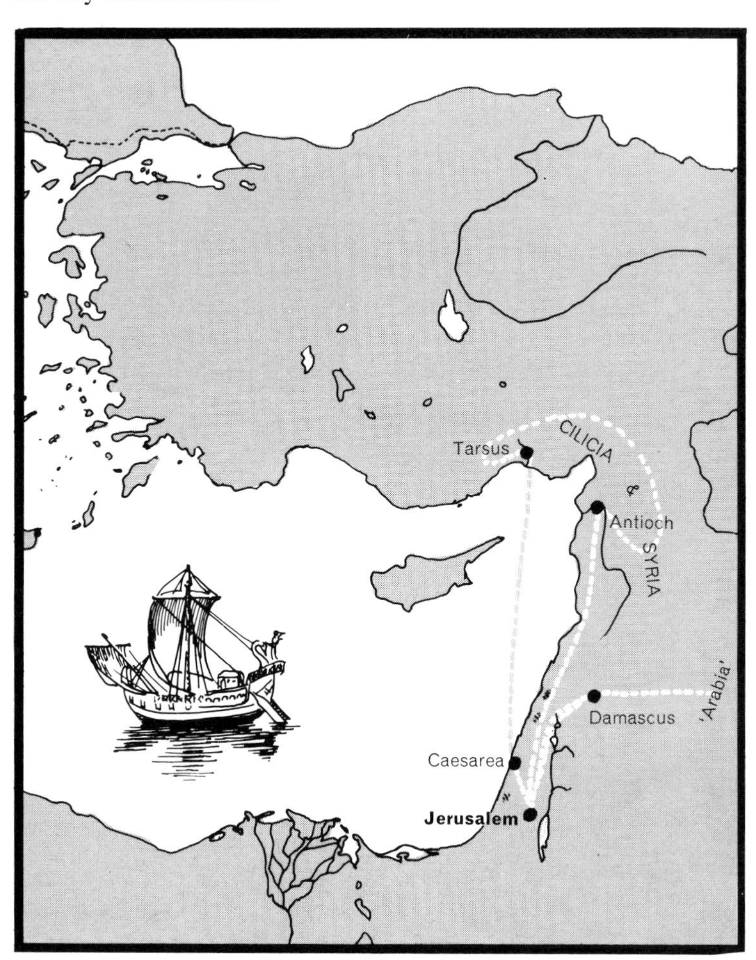

Paul's movements between the time of his Damascus road experience and the Council of Jerusalem.

A Jerusalem to Damascus

B Damascus to 'Arabia'

C Damascus to Jerusalem to Caesarea to Tarsus

D Next 11 years in Cilicia and Syria

E Antioch to Jerusalem

Back to Jerusalem

Acts 9:26–30

Paul now paid a visit to Jerusalem, probably the one described in Galatians 1:18–24. Paul struck terror into the disciples in Jerusalem until Barnabas, one of the leaders of the church, told them of Paul's conversion and witness in Damascus. After this, Paul went out and preached so boldly in Jerusalem itself that the Jews wanted to do away with him. The apostles sent him away to Caesarea for safety, and from there he returned to his original home, in Tarsus. In Galatians Paul explains that his main motive for visiting Jerusalem at this time was to meet Peter, with whom he stayed for fifteen days. He also met James, the brother of Jesus. But he did not meet many of the Christians, and most churches in the area only knew of him by reputation. Paul spent the next eleven years in Cilicia and Syria, probably still unknown to many of the Christians.

Galatians 1:18–19
Galatians 1:22–24

Paul works in Antioch

Acts 11:19–26

Though the Christians in Jerusalem might justifiably have forgotten Paul, Barnabas did not. When he found himself involved in the work of the church in Antioch, in the Roman province of Syria, he sent for Paul and brought him back from Tarsus to help.

Antioch, on the River Orontes, was the third largest city in the Roman world. It was the capital of the Roman province of Syria, and an important centre of commerce. The church at Antioch was fast-growing and dynamic. The town is now Antakya in south-east Turkey.

Paul and Barnabas had been working together for about a year in the church at Antioch when a prophet named Agabus arrived from Jerusalem and declared to the church that a great famine was coming which would affect the Christians in Jerusalem. The church in Antioch decided to send aid to their fellow believers. Barnabas and Paul were to take the relief fund in person. According to Luke, this visit to Jerusalem probably took place in AD 43, when the persecution of Christians in Jerusalem begun by Herod Agrippa I in AD 42 was still going on. It was probably this visit that Paul referred to in Galatians, where the 'revelation' of which he speaks was presumably the prophetic message of Agabus about the famine. Paul says that on this visit he saw the church leaders privately, which is easy to understand if there was persecution going on at the time.

Acts 11:27–30

Galatians 2:1–10

Galatians 2:2

Who were the prophets?

As third largest city of the Roman Empire, Antioch built a reputation for its cultural achievements. The Seleucids and Romans built impressive temples and monuments: this Roman head from Antioch dates from the second century AD.

Opposite. The church at Antioch sent Paul and Barnabas with relief funds to help the Christians in Jerusalem. This early Byzantine building in Antioch has been claimed as the first Christian church.

When Paul was giving advice to the Christians at Corinth about the use of spiritual gifts (*charismata* in Greek) within their church, he advised them to desire all the gifts that had appeared among them, but especially 'prophecy' (1 Corinthians 14:1–5; 12:4–11). What was this prophecy, which we find mentioned in 1 Corinthians and throughout the book of the Acts?

It is clear that there was in the early church an important group of men and women known as prophets. They are frequently listed immediately after the apostles (1 Corinthians 12:28–29; Ephesians 2:20; 3:5; 4:11), while what appear to us to be the more ordinary tasks of evangelist, pastor and teacher are placed after the prophets in order of importance (1 Corinthians 12:28–29; Ephesians 4:11; Acts 13:1; Romans 12:6–8).

These prophets were men and women who had a specially close access to God's will. They could not only forecast certain specific events in the future (as Agabus did, Acts 11:28; 21:10–11; see also Revelation 22:6), but they could also deliver an authentic and authoritative message for a contemporary situation. In Acts 13:1–4, the prophets of the church at Antioch, inspired by the Holy Spirit, gave directions that Paul and Barnabas should be 'set apart . . . for the work to which I have called them'. In the church at Caesarea, the four daughters of Philip the evangelist regularly acted as prophets (Acts 21:8–9). Prophecy also had some connection with the appointment of Timothy (1 Timothy 1:18; 4:14). We also find prophets rebuking Christians who are lazy and encouraging Christians under attack (see for example 1 Corinthians 14:3; Acts 15:32).

Besides such practical activities within the Christian community, the prophet also had an important theological task. In 1 Corinthians 13:2, being a prophet is equated with understanding 'all mysteries and all knowledge'; while Ephesians 3:5–6 makes it clear that the prophet could have a special understanding of God's purposes for the salvation of the Gentiles.

It is difficult for us to appreciate the exact function of these men and women, for we have little with which to compare them. Although there are churches which claim to have prophets today, they usually have different functions from those of New Testament prophets. But it is clear that local congregations of the first century highly regarded the prophets as people who lived in close contact with God, and through whom God could make his will known to the church.

Paul and the Jewish Christians

Galatians 2:1–10

Paul makes it clear that this meeting with the leaders of the Jerusalem church was crucial for his own ministry. At this time the Jerusalem apostles were willing to recognize his mission to the Gentiles as a valid extension of the Christian message. This was an important issue for the early church.

Some Jews, mostly those living in scattered communities in other countries (known as Jews of the 'Dispersion') and Pharisees of the more liberal school of Hillel, had shown considerable missonary zeal in winning converts to Judaism. The Pharisees were great evangelists, willing to 'traverse sea and land to make a single proselyte'. But these converts were required to obey the whole Jewish Law, both ritual and moral. Part of the condition for their full admission to the Jewish faith was the rite of circumcision. (Though it was possible to join in Jewish worship as 'God-fearers' – Cornelius was one of these – without taking upon themselves the whole burden of the Jewish Law.) Naturally the church leaders in Jerusalem, who were still practising Jews, supposed that any Gentiles who wished to become Christians should first become Jews, by being circumcised.

Matthew 23:15

Acts 10:22

Acts 10:1–11:18

The experience of Peter with Cornelius had convinced them that it was possible for a Gentile to be converted and receive the power of the Holy Spirit. But when Paul and Barnabas had a successful mission among the Gentiles in Antioch it was a different matter. For one thing, Cornelius had been an adherent of the Jewish religion as a 'God-fearer', though not as a full proselyte; his case was therefore different from that of complete pagans. In addition, there does not appear to have been a widespread Christian movement connected with Cornelius at the time of Peter's visit; whereas in Antioch a church of Gentile believers was formed. The Jewish Christian leaders were willing to recognize that Paul and Barnabas were engaged in a commendable enterprise, but they refused to accept any responsibility for it.

When Peter later visited Antioch, he at first followed the custom established by Paul, and ate with the Gentile converts. This was something no Jew would normally do, though Peter himself had previously eaten with the family of Cornelius. But when more rigid Jews came from Judea, he gave it up and persuaded Barnabas to do the same. This inconsistency led to a severe rebuke from Paul.

Galatians 2:11–14

This incident is the first example known to us of something that was to trouble Paul throughout his ministry. Although he knew that his own special mission was to Gentiles, Paul could never forget his own race. He was proud of being a Jew. Wherever he went, his first approach was always to the Jews and to those who accepted Judaism. On more than one occasion he raised money for the underprivileged Jewish Christians in Jerusalem. When he came to consider the position of the Jewish race as God's own people, he felt so passionately that he could write: 'I could wish that I myself were accursed and cut off from Christ for the sake of my brethren, my kinsmen by race.' Yet in his

Romans 9:3

Today orthodox Jews still observe detailed regulations concerning food, clothing and Sabbath activity. These male members of a Russian Jewish congregation talk with their Rabbi over cakes and wine.

heart he knew that the Jews were wrong; they had not recognized God's chosen Messiah.

From the beginning of his ministry Paul was an individualist. His commission was unique, just as his conversion had been. But the rumblings of discord first heard in Antioch were to develop into a full peal of thunder in a very short time, as Paul began to fulfil the terms of his calling.

What happened after Paul's conversion?

In our account of what happened after Paul's conversion on the Damascus road, we have taken information from Acts and from Paul's letter to the Galatians. By combining the two sources the order of events emerges as follows:

- Paul's conversion (Acts 9:3–19; 22:6–16; 26:9–18; compare with Galatians 1:11–17).
- A brief stay in Damascus (Acts 9:19b).
- A visit to 'Arabia' (Galatians 1:17).
- Work in Damascus for something like three years (Galatians 1:17; possibly Acts 9:20–22).
- Paul's first visit to Jerusalem after his conversion (Acts 9:26–30; Galatians 1:18–24).
- Paul's stay in Tarsus (Acts 9:30; 11:25; Galatians 1:21).
- Barnabas joins the Christian movement among the Gentiles in Antioch (Acts 11:20–24).
- Paul joins Barnabas in Antioch (Acts 11:25–26).
- Paul and Barnabas visit Jerusalem with famine relief for the church there, fourteen years after Paul's conversion (Acts 11:29–30; 12:25; Galatians 2:1–10).

The view that we have taken here is by no means universally

accepted, especially by German scholars. The question is: Can Paul's own account of his contact with the Jerusalem apostles be reconciled with the account in Acts?

Paul lays great emphasis on the visit which he speaks of in Galatians 2:1–10. He suggests that it was crucial for his entire ministry to the Gentiles. If we look in the book of Acts for an account of a visit which had such significance for Paul's ministry to Gentiles, the occasion which immediately seems to meet this requirement is the one recorded in Acts 15:1–29, when Paul and Barnabas met in council with the other apostles and church leaders to decide once and for all what was to be required of Gentile Christians in relation to the Jewish Law (this is often known as 'the Council of Jerusalem'). The traditional view has therefore been to regard Acts 15:1–29 as an account of the same meeting as Galatians 2:1–10. If this view is accepted, however, two major problems present themselves:

First, according to Acts 15:1–29, the council visit resulted in a thorough and wide-ranging discussion of the very issues with which Paul was dealing when he wrote Galatians. The Council debated the question of Gentile Christians and the Law of the Old Testament. In Acts 15:28–29 we have the details of an agreement worked out by the Council with Paul and Barnabas, and apparently accepted by all as a basis for the admission of Gentiles to the Christian church. Yet in Galatians 2:1–10 Paul makes no reference to any such agreement, even though it would have been crucial in this defence of his own position. In Galatians 2:6 he declares that the Jerusalem church leaders 'added nothing to me', which is a very different story from that in Acts 15, where they insisted that he should conform to the rules they laid down.

Secondly, if Acts 15:1–29 refers to the same events as Galatians 2:1–10, there is an historical discrepancy between the account in Acts and that in Galatians. For between Paul's conversion and the council visit Acts tells of two earlier visits to Jerusalem (Acts 9:26; 11:30; 12:25), while Paul mentions only one (Galatians 1:18). It is inconceivable that Paul could have been mistaken, for the whole of his argument in Galatians would be made invalid if he had omitted to mention even a single meeting. It would therefore be necessary to suppose that Luke must have been mistaken in his account in Acts, either by describing the same incident twice, or out of sheer ignorance of what really happened.

Besides these difficulties in accepting the association of Acts 15:1–29 with Galatians 2:1–10, several smaller points also suggest that in fact these two accounts are not describing the same meeting:

- In Acts 15:2, Paul and Barnabas were 'appointed' by the church at Antioch to go to Jerusalem and meet with 'the apostles and elders'. In Galatians, on the other hand, Paul says that he 'went up by revelation' (Galatians 2:2).
- The conference of Acts 15:1–29 was a semi-public affair, with the apostles and elders and 'the whole church' (15:22). In Galatians, however, Paul makes a special point of mentioning that the meeting was held in private (Galatians 2:2); and only James, Cephas (Peter) and John are mentioned (2:9).
- The outcome of the meeting of Acts 15:1–29 was a decision ('the Apostolic Decree') allowing Gentile converts to remain uncircumcised. It also insisted that they ought to observe certain Jewish dietary customs that would make it easier for Jews to enjoy fellowship with them (Acts 15:28–29). The outcome of the Galatians conference was a mutual

recognition of Paul and Barnabas as apostles to the Gentiles, and of Peter and the others as apostles to the Jews (Galatians 2:9–10).

In view of these differences between Acts 15:1–29 and Galatians 2:1–10, it seems better to suppose that Galatians 2:1–10 records the same events as Acts 11:29–30; 12:25. There are at least four factors in favour of this:

- According to Galatians 2:2, Paul went to Jerusalem 'by revelation'. This expression could well have been intended to denote the prophecy of the famine by Agabus (Acts 11:28).
- Galatians 2:2 suggests that the meeting with the church leaders was a private one. Since Acts dates the famine either during, or shortly after, the persecution of Herod Agrippa I, this could easily explain such secrecy. The absence of James and other Christians from the meeting mentioned in Acts 12:17, which took place during this visit, also supports this reconstruction.
- It is possible to translate Galatians 2:10 as follows: 'Only they asked us to go on remembering the poor, and in fact I had made a special point of doing this very thing.' If this translation is accepted, Paul was in fact making a direct allusion to some such visit as is recorded in Acts 11:25.
- Since Paul obviously intended to recount every visit he made to Jerusalem from the time of his conversion to the time he was writing, if Acts 11:29–30 refers to the same events as Galatians 2:1–10 we can easily explain why he did not mention the Apostolic Decree (which would have been so relevant to his argument in Galatians). The simple fact was that the Apostolic Council had not yet taken place.

On this interpretation, Paul's letter to the Galatians must have been written sometime between the events of Acts 12:25 and Acts 15:1–29. This in turn raises other important questions about the date of Galatians (see chapter 3).

3 Paul Opposes the Legalists

Not long after they had returned from Jerusalem to Antioch, Paul and Barnabas entered a new phase of the work. The Gentile church there, under the guidance of the Holy Spirit, set the two friends apart and sent them off on their first real missionary expedition.

Acts 13:1–3

Cyprus

When they left Antioch, they first went to Cyprus, which was Barnabas' home country. It was there at Paphos, in the record of his interview with the Roman proconsul Sergius Paulus, that we first hear of Paul bringing the Christian message to a Roman official. From this point in Acts, he is always given his Roman name Paul rather than his Hebrew name Saul.

Acts 13:6–12

From Cyprus they sailed to the south coast of Asia Minor, and then crossed the mountains into Pisidia, to another town called Antioch. They then pressed on eastwards to a region called Lycaonia, part of the Roman province of Galatia. After successful missionary work in several towns there they returned to Antioch in Syria by roughly the same route, except that they did not visit Cyprus again.

Acts 13:13–14
Acts 13:51–14:7
Acts 14:7–20
Acts 14:21–28

In each town the apostles began their work in connection with the Jewish synagogue. Probably they felt that in this context they were likely to meet the kind of Gentile 'God-fearers' who would be most open to their message. On the return journey, Paul and Barnabas made a point of revisiting each new congregation of Christians that had been formed, consolidating them in their new faith and appointing elders to be in charge of them.

Acts 14:21–23

At some stage during this expedition Paul fell ill. He refers to a disease which gave him a repulsive appearance when he was visiting the Galatians. We also know that he suffered from a

Galatians 4:13–15

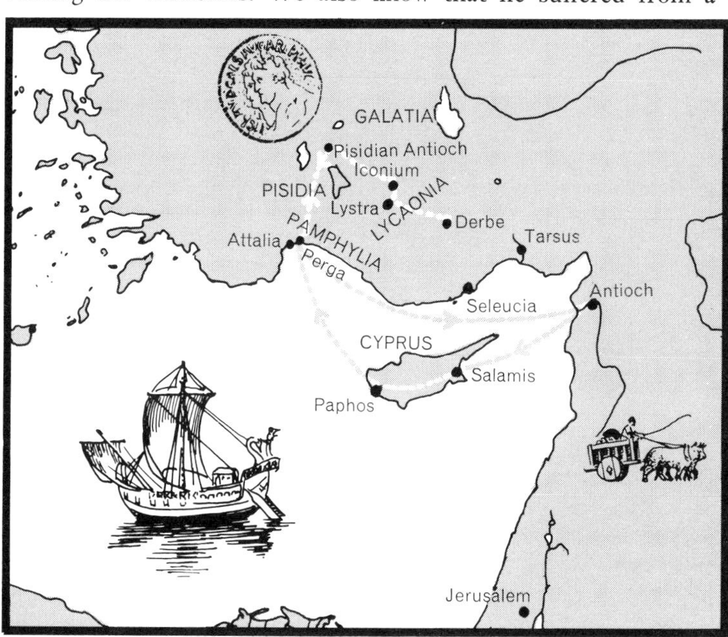

Paul's first missionary journey

Paul and Barnabas' first visit on Cyprus was to Salamis. They started as they meant to continue by preaching first at the Jewish synagogue. The ruins of Salamis, which is near modern Famagusta, include a Roman theatre, harbour and a gymnasium, pictured here.

At Paphos Paul brought the Christian message to the Roman proconsul. These remains may have formed part of his residence, or the forum.

2 Corinthians 12:7

'thorn in the flesh', which is sometimes thought to have been epilepsy. But there is no real evidence that Paul was an epileptic, and the reference in Galatians may well suggest that he had some kind of eye disease.

The first Gentile churches

As a result of Paul's visits, both 'God-fearers' and complete pagans were converted to belief in Jesus Christ. Paul began to realize just how important his own call had been. His experiences at this time also convinced him that Gentile believers should be admitted to the Christian fellowship, without being obliged to be circumcised or to observe other regulations of the Jewish Law. Paul had discovered after his own conversion that his new relationship to Jesus Christ also established a new relationship with other people – including those whom he would otherwise have despised. So now he found that, though he himself had been among the strictest of the Jews, he was united in a new and deeper way with non-Jewish pagans once they too had accepted the claims that Jesus Christ made on their lives. After his experience on the Damascus road, this was what Paul had come to expect. It had been made clear to him then that he was to fulfil a very special role in spreading the Christian message to all men throughout

Antioch in Pisidia, high in what is now central Turkey, was a Roman city with a strong Hellenistic Greek and Jewish culture – just the sort of place Paul chose for his visits. The aqueduct once carried by these arches provided Antioch's water-supply.

the world. When Paul and Barnabas returned to Syrian Antioch, they found that the church there agreed with them on this point, and welcomed their success in evangelizing the peoples of southern Asia Minor.

Acts 14:27–28

Jews and Gentiles

Galatians 2:11–14

But this happy situation did not last long. Messengers from the Jerusalem church soon arrived in Antioch with a very different attitude. What was worse, they also visited the new congregations of Christians which Paul and Barnabas had just formed on their first missionary expedition. They began to cause havoc among these new Christians by telling them that Paul had only told them half the Christian message. According to Paul, if Gentiles were willing to accept the claims of Christ over their lives they would be given power by the Holy Spirit working within them to live the kind of life that was pleasing to God. To many Jewish Christians, this idea was blasphemous. They believed that God had revealed his will in the Old Testament, where it was clearly taught that in order to be a part of the divine community a person must be circumcised and observe many other regulations. How could Paul claim that these Gentiles were proper Christians when they had never even considered the full implications of

It was through country like this that Paul and Barnabas travelled during their first missionary journey. This part of the Turkish central highlands is near Pisidian Antioch.

God's Old Testament revelation? How dare he suggest that Christian morality could be attained by any means other than a strict application of Jewish rules and regulations to the life of the Christian?

The new converts were thrown into confusion by such teaching. All they knew was that they had accepted the message Paul declared; that their lives had been revolutionized by the same Lord whom Paul had met on the Damascus road; and that they were to trust that Lord to help them live lives that were pleasing to God. Many of them had never been followers of the Jewish religion, and had no idea what was in the Old Testament. Paul had given them no indication that it was necessary for them

After preaching in Perga, Paul and Barnabas completed their first missionary journey by sailing back from Attalia to Syrian Antioch. There they recounted their experiences to the church which had commissioned them. Attalia is now the modern resort of Antalya in southern Turkey.

to find out in order to be acceptable to God.

But when these new Christians began to read the Old Testament under the guidance of these Jewish Christians, they found themselves faced with a mass of rules and regulations which they knew they could never hope to fulfil, even if it was necessary to do so for salvation. Some of them decided to make a brave attempt, and began by keeping the Jewish sabbath and possibly certain other Jewish festivals as well. A large number of them began to think about being circumcised, in order to fulfil what seemed to be the requirements of the Old Testament. But the great majority simply did not know what to do.

Galatians 4:8–11

Galatians 5:2–12

It was at this point that news of the situation reached Paul. He

was naturally infuriated by what he heard. It was impossible for him to visit these churches again just at that time, so in the heat of the moment he decided that he must write a letter to them. This was the letter known to us as the letter to the Galatians.

Paul's letters

Acts 23:26–30

When Paul wrote letters to the Christians who were under his care, he naturally followed the common style of the day. We have an example in Claudias Lysias' letter to Felix. An ancient letter usually followed a more or less set pattern:

- It always began with the name of the writer, and then named the person it was sent to. Paul follows this quite closely.
- Then follows the greeting, usually a single word. But Paul often expanded this to include the traditional Hebrew greeting (*shalōm*, 'peace') together with a new, Christian greeting ('grace' – in Greek very similar to the normal everyday greeting).
- The third part of a Greek letter was a polite expression of thanks for the good health of the person addressed. This is usually expanded by Paul into a general thanksgiving to God for all that was praiseworthy in his readers.
- Next followed the main body of the letter. In Paul's letters this is often divided into two parts: doctrinal teaching (often in response to questions raised by his readers) and then a moral plea for Christian living.
- Personal news and greetings came next. In Paul's case this is more often news of the churches and prominent individuals in them.
- There is often also in Paul's letters a note of exhortation or blessing in his own handwriting, as a kind of guarantee of the genuine and personal nature of the letter.
- Finally, ancient letters often ended with a single word of farewell. Paul almost always expands this into a full blessing and prayer for his readers.

Paul writes to the Galatian churches

Galatians 1:1–2
Galatians 1:3
Galatians 1:4–5

A quick look at Galatians will show us just how closely Paul kept to this pattern, even when he was writing what must have been a very hurried letter. He begins by giving his own name: 'Paul an apostle'; and he associates with his letter 'all the brethren who are with me'. The people to whom he was writing are then named, in this case a group of churches: 'the churches of Galatia'. The greeting follows, 'grace . . . and peace', and is expanded into a brief sentence of praise to God.

One very significant omission is to be noted at this point. Nowhere in Galatians does Paul give thanks for the spiritual condition of his readers. There was nothing to be thankful for. They had not been Christians long enough for Paul to be able to refer to praiseworthy deeds done in the past (as he does, for example, in Philippians 1:3–11). And their condition at the moment of writing certainly gave Paul no cause for thanksgiving.

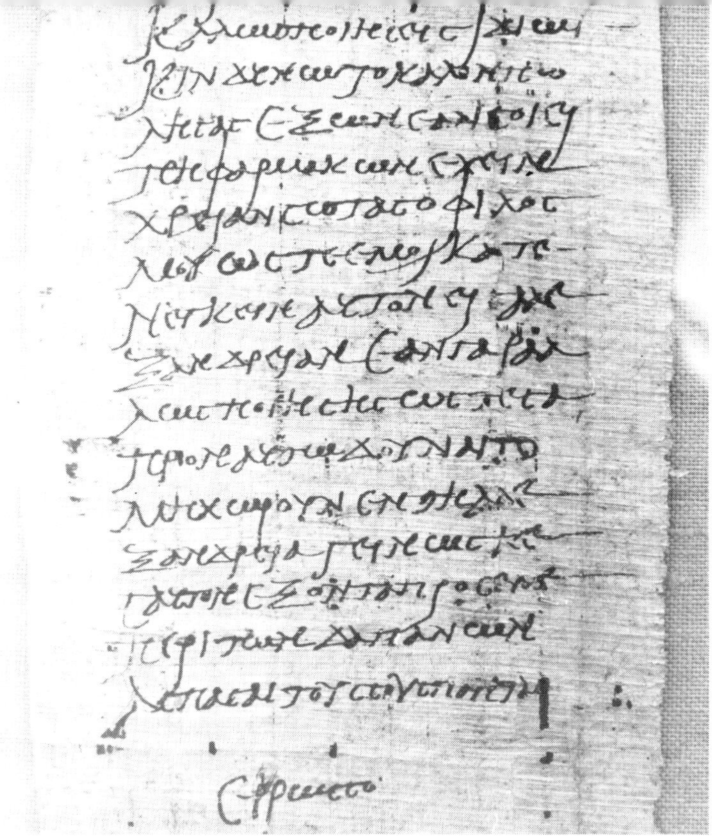

Paul wrote to many of the churches which he had founded or visited. This example of a letter on papyrus was written in Greek in the first century AD and opens 'Prokleios to his good friend Pekysis, greetings.'

The main body of the letter now follows. It is divided roughly into a doctrinal and theoretical section, from 1:6 to 4:31; and a practical description of Christian living from 5:1 to 6:10. No personal news and greetings finish this letter. Paul had no time for such pleasantries. But he does make a final appeal in his own handwriting. This supplies the interesting information that his own writing was much larger than that of the secretary who had written most of the letter – an observation which, incidentally, gives added probability to the suggestion that Paul may have suffered from bad eyesight. Paul ends his letter with a blessing which was also a prayer for his readers, and assures them that a power greater than their own is ready to their hand: 'The grace of our Lord Jesus Christ be with your spirit, brethren, Amen.'

Galatians 6:11–17

Galatians 6:18

Who were the Galatians?

In our earlier discussion of the order of events following Paul's conversion, it was suggested that the letter to the Galatians is to be dated about AD 48, written just before the visit of Paul and Barnabas to Jerusalem for the Apostolic Council. The arguments set out there are solid evidence for accepting this early date. On this reckoning Galatians would be the first letter that Paul ever wrote, and probably therefore the first part of the New Testament to be written. But what we have said so far is only half the story.

In addressing the letter, Paul says he is writing 'to the churches of Galatia' (Galatians 1:2); and he calls his readers Galatians (3:1). Now the mention of people who could be called 'Galatians' would most naturally suggest the Celtic people of that name who lived in the region of Ankara in

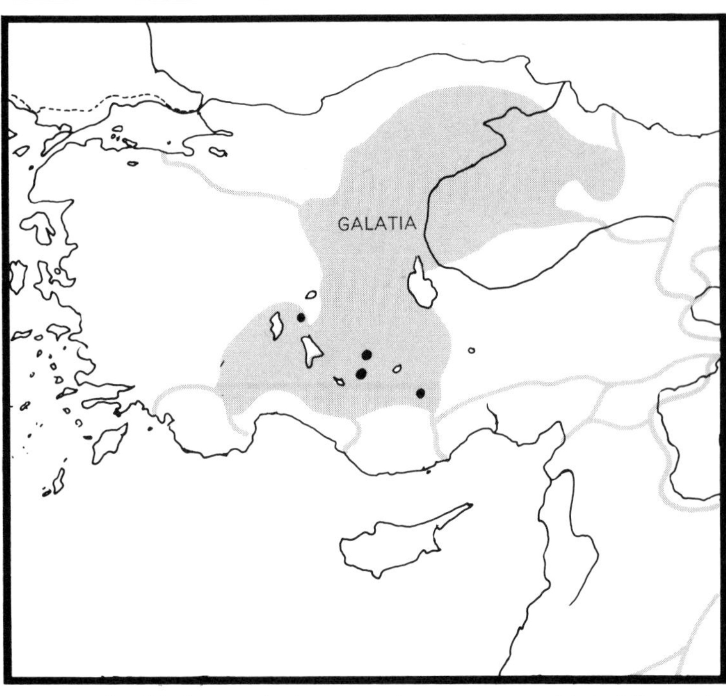

The location of Galatia

present-day Turkey, and who gave their name to an ancient kingdom there. The problem is that if these are the people referred to, we know from Acts that Paul did not visit them until his second and third missionary expeditions (Acts 16:6; 18:23). In that case he could not have written to them as early as AD 48.

It has also been argued that Paul's teaching in Galatians closely resembles what he says in Romans, and without doubt Romans was written towards the end of his third missionary tour. Is it not therefore more reasonable to suppose that this letter was written to the people of north Galatia some time between AD 56 and 58? This view is in fact widely held, and the dating suggested in this book is a minority view, though one that has been, and continues to be, held by many very eminent scholars.

Sir William Ramsay was the first scholar of any importance to put forward the view adopted here. At the beginning of this century, he engaged in extensive archaeological investigations in the very areas of Asia Minor of which we are speaking. In the course of his work he discovered that the *Roman province* of Galatia included not only the ancient kingdom of the Galatians in the north of Asia Minor, but also the southern region of Lycaonia ('south Galatia'), in which Paul had preached during his first missionary expedition and where he had established churches at Lystra, Derbe and Iconium. If we accept Ramsay's evidence, we have strong support for the viewpoint adopted here – that Galatians was written about AD 48 to the churches Paul had visited on his first missionary expedition.

The other argument put forward to support a later date for the letter (that it is similar to Romans) is weak. It is based on the subjective comparison of two documents. The evidence which led the great nineteenth-century scholar, J. B. Lightfoot, to give a late date to Galatians can just as easily be interpreted in a completely different way to support an early date for the letter!

Galatians

That has covered only the bare bones of the letter. The more important question is, what was Paul actually saying? Though Galatians is not an especially long and involved letter, it is not always very easy to understand Paul's meaning. This is partly because the letter was written hastily in the middle of a raging controversy. In such circumstances no man expresses himself in the ordered way he would in calmer moments. The complexity of his expression also stems partly from his subject-matter. For Paul was as much at home in the Old Testament as we are in our daily newspapers. He quotes it with great freedom as he sets out to expound the twin principles of liberty and equality within the Christian fellowship.

Paul's letter falls conveniently into three main sections. He deals in turn with three false ideas that had been propounded by the Jewish Christians ('Judaizers') who had visited the Galatian churches.

Did Paul have any authority?

The first thing the Judaizers had said was that Paul was not a proper apostle. Because he had not been accredited by the original apostles in Jerusalem, he had no right to give any directions to new Christians, nor ought they to pay attention to what he said. We find Paul's reply to all this in Galatians 1:10–2:21. He makes it quite clear that he needed no authorization from Jerusalem or anywhere else, since he had himself met with the risen Christ

The other apostles (except James, who had a similar experience to Paul, see 1 Corinthians 15:7) had all been disciples of Jesus during his ministry. But Paul was not inferior on that account, for he too had a face-to-face encounter with Jesus. It was this meeting that gave him his authorization as an apostle (Galatians 1:11–12). He had indeed visited Jerusalem on several occasions, but on none of them had he felt it necessary to obtain the permission of the original disciples to carry on his work, nor had they suggested that he needed such permission (1:18–2:10).

In fact, quite the opposite was the case; for, Paul says, 'when they saw that I had been entrusted with the gospel to the uncircumcised (or non-Jews), just as Peter had been entrusted with the gospel to the circumcised (the Jews) . . . and when they perceived the grace that was given to me (by my encounter with the risen Christ), James and Cephas and John . . . gave to me and Barnabas the right hand of fellowship, that we should go to the Gentiles and they to the circumcised' (Galatians 2:7–9).

The events at Antioch proved conclusively that Paul was in no way inferior to Peter (Cephas), commonly reckoned to be the greatest of the apostles. When Peter had broken off eating with Gentile Christians at Antioch, merely because some Jewish believers arrived from Jerusalem, Paul had no hesitation in opposing him 'to his face' (2:11). So far as we know Peter accepted the rebuke delivered to him on that occasion.

Christians and the Old Testament

After he has dealt with this malicious attack on his own credentials, Paul appeals briefly to the Galatians' own experience before going on to deal with the second piece of false teaching propounded by the Jewish intruders. What they knew of Christ ought to have shown them that they had received the Holy Spirit (the mark of the true Christian, Romans 8:9) not because they had obeyed the Old Testament Law, but because they had exercised faith in Jesus (Galatians 3:1–5).

This leads straight into an attack on another part of their teachings. In the Old Testament the promise of the Messianic kingdom was given to Abraham and his descendants (Genesis 17:7–8). *Therefore the Judaizers argued that anyone who wished to be in the Messianic kingdom must become members of Abraham's family by circumcision and continued obedience to the Old Testament Law* (Genesis 17:9–14). Paul answers this in three ways, by appealing to the Old Testament itself:

● In Galatians 3:6–14, he points out that the blessings promised to Abraham belong to 'men of faith' (verse 9). Abraham had faith in God, and this faith was the basis of his acceptance by God (Genesis 12:1–4; see also Hebrews 11:8–12; 17–18). At the same time, 'all who rely on works of the law are under a curse' (verse 10). Everyday experience and the Old Testament both proved that in practice it was impossible to be justified in God's sight by keeping the Law.

● But was not the Law God's highest revelation in the Old Testament, surpassing all that had gone before it? No, says Paul. Since the Law (or Torah) came into effect long after Abraham's time, it could not possibly alter a direct promise made to him by God. The 'inheritance' promised to Abraham could not be obtainable by both Law and promise (verse 18). The Law had a rather different purpose in God's plan:

First, the Law served to show up sin as a transgression against God (Galatians 3:19; see also Romans 4:15; 5:13). Before it was given, the only law that humans had was the 'law of nature' expressing itself through their own conscience. After the Law was given by Moses, people saw wrongdoing for what it really was – defiance against God's will.

Secondly, the Law was given to be men's teacher 'until Christ came, that we might be justified by faith' (Galatians 3:24). Men tried to gain salvation by their own efforts at keeping the Law, but they realized that it was an impossible task. So the way was prepared for God's new act of grace in Jesus Christ.

● Paul now takes the argument to its logical conclusion (Galatians 3:25–4:7). The Old Testament Law was only effective 'till the offspring should come to whom the promise had been made' (verse 19) The 'offspring' *had* come in Jesus Christ. So the era of the Law was now finished, and to those who had faith in him, Christ would give freedom from the Law. Before they had been slaves to 'the elemental spirits of the universe' (which included the Law, 4:3). Now they were sons and heirs of the promise made to Abraham (4:4–7).

Freedom and legalism

By trying to put themselves under the Law and keeping the Jewish holy days, the Galatians were really trying to undo what God had already done for them in Christ. Paul was fearful that if they did this, he had laboured over them in vain (4:8–11). So he goes on to deal with another argument put forward by the Judaizing teachers. They had given 'scriptural' reasons to suggest that Christians ought to keep the Torah and to be circumcised. Paul answers in three ways:

● Paul looks again at the status of the Law (4:21–5:1). Again he appeals to the story of Abraham, this time using the incident of Sarah (a free woman) driving out Hagar the slave. This, he says, is an allegory of the superior position of the good news in Christ over against the legalism of the Jewish Law.

● Paul answers the queries about circumcision (5:2–12). He makes it clear that circumcision is of no value either way to the Christian. It makes no difference whether the Christian is circumcised or not. His standing before God depends not on this kind of external sign but on 'faith working through love' (5:6). In the case of people like the Galatians, to submit to circumcision would actually be a denial of what Christ had done for them (5:2). In any case, to be circumcised also obliged a man to observe the whole of the Jewish Law (5:3). This was the very thing that Paul had just rejected, and which experience showed to be impossible anyway. The freedom that Christ brings is clearly incompatible with the 'yoke of slavery' (5:1) brought by circumcision and the Law.

● Paul deals with the problem of Christian behaviour (Galatians 5:13–6:10). One thing that marked the Jews off from other peoples in the ancient world was their very high moral standards, which came as a result of their close adherence to the Old Testament Law. The false teachers who visited Galatia had argued that if Christians did not follow the Jewish Law, they would have no guide for their conduct. They would be indistinguishable from the pagans around them. This was an important question, and one that was not easy to answer.

Paul had told the Galatian Christians that, if they accepted the risen Christ as Lord over their lives, the Holy Spirit would reproduce within them the life of Christ himself. This is the kind of thing he indicated in 2:20: 'I have been crucified with Christ; it is no longer I who live, but Christ who lives in me; and the life I now live in the flesh I live by faith in the Son of God who loved me and gave himself for me.'

Paul deals with the accusations of the Judaizers on this score by making four important statements:

First (5:13–15), 'freedom' in Christ does not mean a freedom to do what we like. It is a freedom to serve one another in love. Since the Holy Spirit aims to produce in Christians a Christ-like character, their freedom should obviously be demonstrated in ways that are consistent with this.

Secondly (5:16–26), though the Christian gospel does not lay down a list of do's and don'ts, 'those who belong to Christ Jesus have crucified the flesh with its passions and desires' (5:24). So the Christian's life will be marked out by the fruit of the Spirit. The demands of Christ are far more radical than those of a religion that only imposes rules and regulations from the outside. The Christian's whole personality has been revolutionized. His attitudes and behaviour have been changed from within. This was the same lesson that Jesus himself had taught: 'A sound tree cannot bear evil fruit, nor can a bad tree bear good fruit' (Matthew 7:18).

Thirdly (6:1–6), Christians should beware of judging others. They ought to recognize that they themselves could have no moral strength to do what was right, apart from the power of the Holy Spirit. They are to 'fulfil the law of Christ' by bearing 'one another's burdens' (6:2). This is very different from keeping externally imposed rules and regulations by their own efforts.

Fourthly (6:7–10), Paul sums up his advice. In order to reap the harvest of eternal life, they must sow not to the flesh – their own self-gratification – but to the Spirit – their new life given by Jesus Christ.

Then finally, in Galatians 6:11–18, Paul makes his last appeal to his readers. He makes two further points against his opponents; then he makes two balancing statements of his own belief and practice.

His opponents, in spite of their high pretensions, were in fact spiritually bankrupt (6:12). They 'want to make a good showing in the flesh', the very thing that Paul had denounced in the previous section of his argument (Galatians 6:8: 'he who sows to his own flesh will from the flesh reap corruption'). They are also inconsistent, even with their own starting-points; though they emphasize the outward sign of circumcision they are not willing to accept the spiritual discipline involved in keeping the Old Testament Law.

Paul knew that the truth revealed to him by the risen Christ was greater than anything else. So he says finally that the only real cause of boasting before God is that the Christian has been crucified to the world, through the cross of Christ.

When someone spoke of a cross in the first century, he meant only one thing – death. That is what Paul means when he writes of

Christians sharing in the cross of Christ (Galatians 2:20). He is not urging them to be martyrs. But he is saying that Christians must die to themselves. They must give up their claims over their lives, and accept Jesus Christ as Saviour and Lord over every aspect of life. This kind of 'new creation' is the only thing of any value in the sight of God, and forms the sole qualifying mark of 'the Israel of God' (Galatians 6:14–16). Paul himself may be criticized because he is a Jewish deserter. But he has the mark of true spirituality before God: 'I bear on my body the marks of Jesus' (6:17).

This, then, is how Paul dealt with the problems of the churches of Galatia. If we want a slogan to sum it all up, and indeed to sum up the whole of Paul's conviction, we can find it in Galatians 6:15: 'in Christ, it is not circumcision or uncircumcision that counts, but the power of a new birth.'

The Apostolic Council

Acts 15:6–21

Acts 15:6–11

No doubt it was in this fashion that Paul set out his arguments at the Council of Jerusalem in AD 49. According to Acts even James, probably the most Jewish of the Jerusalem leaders, had to accept the truth of the main part of Paul's argument. The Jerusalem apostles agreed that there was no great doctrinal principle involved. But there was still the simple, practical problem of how Jews and Gentiles could meet together at the same table (including the communion table).

In order to make this possible the Jewish leaders suggested that Gentile converts should abstain from those activities that were particularly offensive to Jewish Christians: things like eating food that had been offered in pagan sacrifices, eating meat from which the blood had not been drained, or practising pagan marriage habits which did not accord with the Jewish Law and custom.

Acts 15:19–21; 28–29

This arrangement was accepted by Paul. But it was a compromise, and a compromise solution is hardly ever very successful. This one appears to have been no exception, for when Paul came to face the same problems over again in Corinth, he did not refer to the terms of the Apostolic Decree at all, but argued once more from the basic principles involved in the matter.

1 Corinthians 8:1–13; 10:19–11:1

Why did Paul accept the Council's Decree?

There is another problem with the Apostolic Decree, however, which is not explained quite so easily. We must face the fact that if Paul had written Galatians just before he went to the Council, the narrative of Acts 15 depicts him accepting something that he had vehemently rejected in Galatians – the application of some sort of 'law' to Gentile Christians.

One solution to this problem has been *to suppose that the Apostolic Council never actually happened*. This view suggests it was invented by Luke for the purpose of showing that both Jewish and Gentile sections of the church were united in the early years of its history. It is largely the result of supposing that the narrative of Acts cannot be reconciled with Galatians 1–2. We have already seen that this is no real difficulty. So we need not suppose that Luke was either unknowingly or deliberately falsifying the record when he wrote of the Council. We have also noticed that in those areas where his story can be tested by external evidence, Luke emerges as a first-class historian. We have no reason to suspect his reliability at this point on general historical grounds.

Another possibility is *to suppose that the Apostolic Decree was in fact addressed to just a small and relatively local group of churches*, namely those mentioned in Acts 15:36–16:5. If this was the case, there would be no difficulty over the fact that Paul did not quote the Decree in 1 Corinthians.

Perhaps a better explanation is simply that *Paul was at heart a conciliatory sort of man*. Having said his piece in Galatians, and having won the theological debate in Jerusalem, he was content to accept that regardless of theological differences Jews and Gentiles had to live together within the local church, and the acceptance of these guidelines was a simple means of achieving this.

As we go on to look at Paul's experiences in other churches, we will see that time and again he bent over backwards to accommodate people whose viewpoint was different from his own (see also 1 Corinthians 9:19–23). He realized that a divided church was a poor witness to the non-Christian world, and at this stage of his ministry the Apostolic Decree seemed the best solution to a pressing problem.

4 Paul the Missionary

AFTER his crucial meeting with the leaders of the Jerusalem church, Paul went off again into the Gentile world fired with a new enthusiasm. He was determined to revolutionize the Roman Empire in the name of Jesus Christ.

He began his second expedition with a new companion. Barnabas did not go along because Paul was unwilling to give a second chance to John Mark, Barnabas' cousin who had deserted them during their first expedition. But Paul found a keen helper in Silas, one of the men sent to Antioch to explain the decisions of the Jerusalem Council to the church there. In the course of his expedition, he was to acquire two other companions in addition to Silas: Timothy, who joined them at Lystra, and Luke who joined them at Troas.

Acts 15:36–40
Acts 15:30–33
Acts 16:1–3
Acts 16:10–12

Back to Galatia

The first thing Paul did on this tour was to revisit some of the congregations which he had founded in south Galatia during his first expedition from Antioch. He had been wanting to see them ever since he heard of the interference of the Judaizers in their congregations. During this further visit he no doubt explained that, although as Christians they were free from all the legal requirements of the Jewish Law, it would be desirable if they could agree to accept the arrangement that had been worked out in Jerusalem. In this way Jewish Christians could feel free to meet with them.

Acts 16:4

After this, Paul and Silas went on with Timothy, who had joined them in Lystra, through Phrygia and Galatia – perhaps this time north Galatia. Paul had planned to go to the Roman province of Asia, the area round Ephesus in the west of Asia Minor, and also into Bithynia, the province to the north which adjoined the Black Sea. But both these intentions were expressly forbidden by the Holy Spirit (we do not know by what means). So Paul and his companions went on into Troas, ancient Troy, in the part of Asia Minor nearest to Europe.

Acts 16:6
Acts 16:6–7

Forward into Europe

Acts 16:9–10

During the night Paul had a dream of a Macedonian appealing for help. This was recognized by Paul as a directive from God to cross the Aegean Sea into Europe. This was not the first time that Christian missionaries had gone into Europe, for at a later date Paul wrote to a large and flourishing church at Rome, which had not been founded by his own efforts. But Paul's entry into Europe at this point was a distinct step forward in the achievement of his desire to spread the good news of Jesus throughout the whole of the Roman Empire.

Philippi

Acts 16:13

The first town the missionaries visited was Philippi. This was a Roman colony in the north-east corner of Macedonia, largely populated by retired soldiers from the Roman army. Although the city had such a large Gentile population, Paul still followed his earlier custom of first going to the Jews at their usual meeting-place, in this case simply called 'a place of prayer' by the riverside. There were so few Jews in Philippi that they did not even have a synagogue building.

Among Paul's hearers at this place of prayer was Lydia, and she was the first one to become a Christian in Philippi. If Paul had any doubts about abandoning his earlier plans and moving in-

Bottom. Paul was summoned to Europe by a dream in which a Macedonian (a man from northern Greece) appealed to him. This Latin inscription from Philippi includes the name of the Roman province of Macedonia.

Paul's second missionary journey

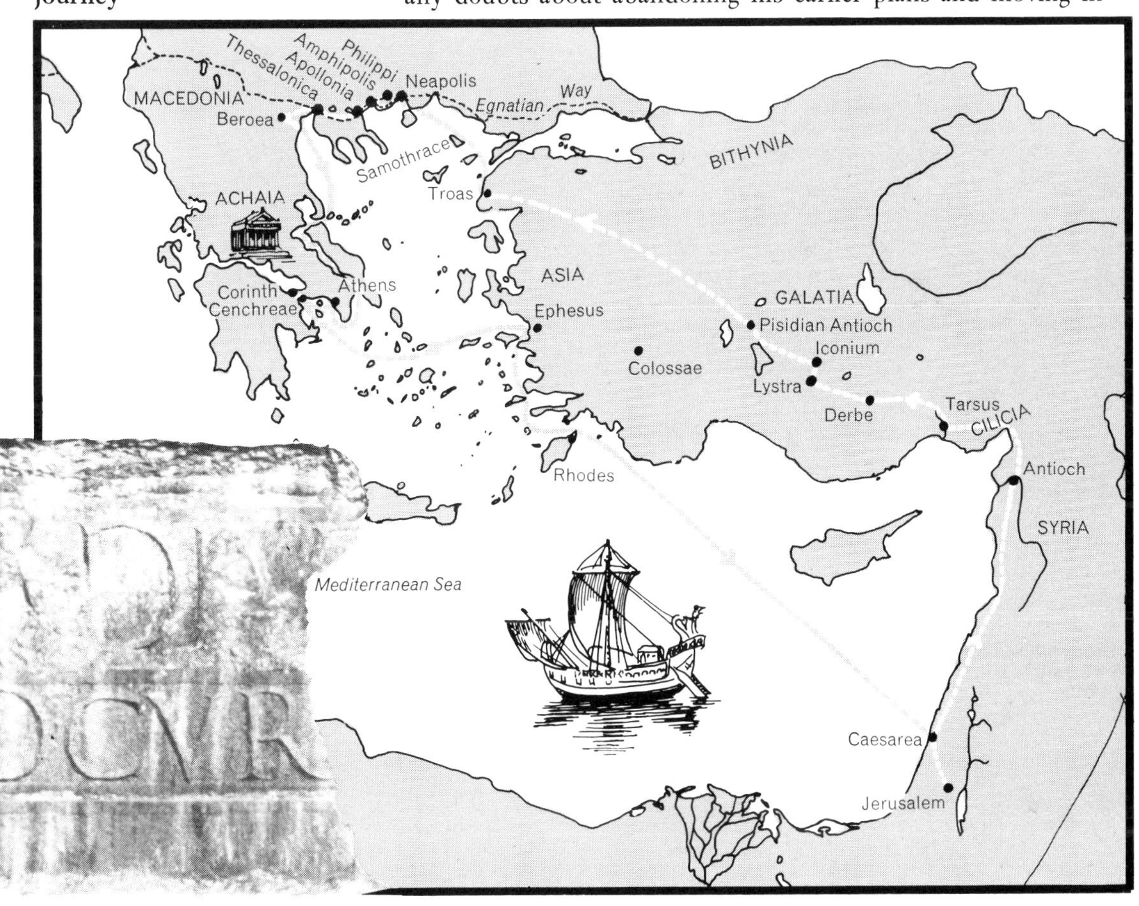

stead into Europe, they must have disappeared with the conversion of this woman. She was a native of Thyatira, a city in the very area of Asia Minor where Paul had been intending to go. She may well have been the one who first took the Christian message to her home town, where there was soon a large Christian church. In any event, her belief in Jesus Christ clearly made a revolutionary change in her life. Though she was a woman of some importance, her own home was soon opened to Paul and his friends and became the headquarters of their activity. Once again it was demonstrated that belief in Jesus Christ created a unity of fellowship between men and women that overthrew all normal social and racial barriers.

Revelation 2:18–29

One thing that happened at Philippi gives us a good illustration of some of the reasons why the Christian faith aroused so much antagonism in many parts of the Roman Empire at this time. As he was going about his evangelistic work, Paul was continually pestered by a slave girl who, by means of some kind of second sight exercised in trances, had brought a large income to her owners.

Paul knew that Jesus had promised to give 'release to the captives'; and he had declared clearly that Christians could be released from captivity to the Jewish Law, and from bondage to the social distinctions of the day. Surely Christ's apostles should act in his name to release a girl like this from slavery to her owners and to the demons who were believed to possess her? Jesus had already overcome the very powers of evil which had reduced her to this condition. So Paul cured her of the spirit of divination in the name of Christ. At this, her owners were so angry that they accused Paul and Silas of creating a public disturbance by recommending customs that were unlawful for Roman citizens.

Acts 16:16–18

Acts 16:19–21

Paul in prison

Accusing someone of causing a public nuisance could always be guaranteed to arouse a Roman official to some sort of action. This occasion was no exception. Paul and Silas were flogged and thrown into prison. They had shown a slave girl the way to a new freedom in Christ, only to lose their own freedom. Not that they worried about that, for they spent the night singing praises to God for his goodness to them.

During the night an earthquake broke open the prison doors. Though they could have escaped, they chose to remain, along with the rest of the prisoners. Their jailor was ready to kill himself, thinking they had already escaped. But when confronted with the messengers of Christ he realized that they were men with an inner dynamic he did not possess. He immediately asked the secret of their power, and became a Christian himself, along with his family.

After the conversion of this man Paul knew that there was no need for him to remain in prison. In fact he ought never to have

As Roman colonists, the Philippians had the same rights and privileges as the Italians themselves. This Latin inscription includes the city's name.

been there in the first place, for he was a Roman citizen. Paul therefore claimed his rights as a citizen, demanding from the city authorities an apology for the illegal beating he had suffered. Then he left the city of Philippi altogether.

Acts 16:22–40

Luke stayed in Philippi to look after the new Christians. They came from all levels of society and included a prominent local trader, a soothsayer who looked for business in the main streets, and the town's jailor and his family. Small wonder that at one of the next places they visited Paul, Silas and Timothy were described as 'men who have turned the world upside down'.

Acts 17:6

The next towns the three friends came to were Thessalonica and Beroea, in both of which there were large Jewish communities. In both places many converts were made, and in both there was severe opposition from the Jews. This seems to have been directed specifically at Paul himself, as a former Pharisee, since Silas and Timothy were able to stay on there when Paul went on to Athens.

Acts 17:4–15

The great Roman roads were of vital military and commercial importance. The stone slabs of the Egnatian Way were worn down by the heavy traffic. Paul's group used this route to travel on from Philippi to Thessalonica.

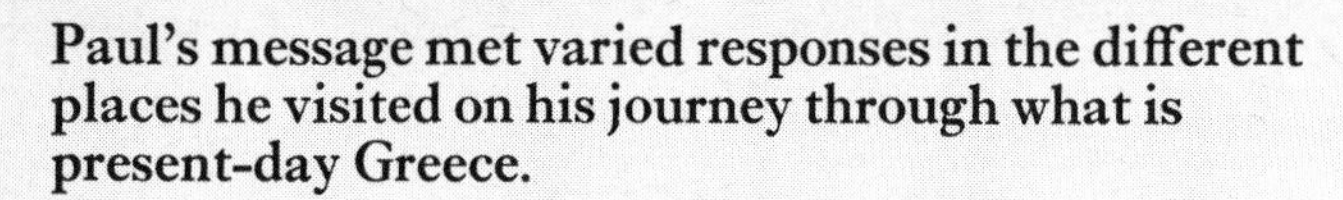

Paul's message met varied responses in the different places he visited on his journey through what is present-day Greece.

During his second missionary journey Paul revisited many of the places where he had previously been, and travelled hundreds of miles across the mountains of what is now central Turkey.

Paul first set foot in Europe at Neapolis, the modern port of Kavalla in northern Greece. Neapolis stood at the terminus of the Egnatian Way, the military road connecting Rome with the east. From Neapolis he went to Philippi, leading city of the district.

Athens symbolized the tradition of classical learning. The Acropolis, on which the Parthenon was built as a temple to the goddess Athene, served as both a focus of worship and a defensive stronghold.

Philippi was an important Roman colony standing on the Egnatian Way. Its citizens fostered great civic pride. It was a largely Gentile city, and in Paul's time the 'God-fearers' used to meet by the river bank.

Corinth, like Athens, was dominated by a stronghold built on a steep rock above the city. In the foreground is the Tribunal, near to which stood the other principal public buildings, including the theatre and *agora*.

Athens

So Paul arrived in Athens, the intellectual centre of the ancient world. By this time it had lost its former claims to political greatness. But it was still a university town to which many young Romans were sent to study philosophy or to be initiated into one of the many oriental Mystery Religions which found a home there. The Athenians still liked to have a good debate. When the news got around that the teacher of a new religion had arrived from the east, Paul was called before the court of the Areopagus, which evidently believed that taking an interest in philosophy was part of its job of ruling the city.

Acts 17:22–31
Acts 14:15–17

In speaking at Athens to people who had no Jewish or biblical background at all, Paul adopted a completely different approach from his earlier work. However, it is comparable with the way he had addressed pagans in Lystra. When addressing Jews and Gentile 'God-fearers', Paul could begin from the Old Testament and point out how the promises made there had been fulfilled in the life, death and resurrection of Jesus. At Athens, he began from the more-or-less Greek view of God as creator, benefactor and 'presence' within the universe. He then went on to speak of the human search for God, who is 'not far from each one of us', a statement which he supported by quotations from the Greek poets Epimenides and Aratus.

Acts 17:27

Acts 17:29–31

Acts 7:48–50

Paul condemned as a form of ignorance the idolatry which he saw in Athens, with arguments that had been used in philosophical Greek thought since the days of Xenophanes in the sixth century BC. The same kind of arguments had also been used by Jewish missionaries when they spoke in support of their own faith in one God, and we can see here several resemblances to the teaching of the early Christian evangelist Stephen.

Acts 17:30

Acts 17:34

Having condemned idolatry, Paul went on to call his hearers to repentance and the worship of the one true God. So far everything would be received sympathetically by many of his Greek audience. In concluding his address, Paul referred to the coming judgement of the world, of which he said an assurance had been given in the fact that God raised Jesus from the dead. At this point, the Athenians were either amused or annoyed by what he said. It was not the Platonic doctrine of the immortality of the soul that Paul was preaching, but the Jewish belief in the resurrection of the body, something absurd and abhorrent to intelligent Greeks. Even so there were a few converts at Athens.

Paul opened his address to the Court of the Areopagus by referring to an altar dedicated to an 'unknown god'. This example of a similar altar stands in the Palatine Gardens, Rome, and dates from the period of the Roman Republic in the century before Christ.

Opposite. The Court of the Areopagus, where Paul was called on to speak, met in one of the colonnaded buildings surrounding the market-place (*agora*) in the foreground. Overlooking the *agora* are the Acropolis (centre) and Areopagus (sometimes known as Mars Hill) from which the court took its name.

Corinth

Paul now pressed on to Corinth, an ancient Greek city that had been rebuilt as a Roman colony in 46 BC. It was a prosperous trading centre, and also had a name for permitting vice of every kind.

Acts 18:11

Paul made Corinth the headquarters of his work for Christ for the next eighteen months. While he was there he made friends with Aquila and his wife Priscilla who, like himself, were tent-makers. As before, he began his work in the Jewish synagogue, but left when he met the usual Jewish opposition, dramatically shaking out his clothes before doing so. He then started preaching from the home of a new Christian, Titius Justus, who lived next door to the synagogue. As a result of Paul's work, many inhabitants of Corinth became Christians, including Crispus, one of the synagogue rulers. A very large and influential Christian congregation was established in the city.

Acts 18:7

Acts 18:8

Paul and Gallio

After Paul had been there for about eighteen months, the Jews decided to make a concerted effort to have him convicted of some crime. There was a new Roman magistrate, the proconsul Gallio, who was brother of the Roman poet-philosopher, Seneca. The charge failed, because Gallio would not judge Paul under the Jewish Law, and according to Roman law he had committed no crime. This is one of the incidents in Paul's life that we can date fairly precisely. The period of Gallio's office in Corinth is recorded in a copy of a letter sent from the emperor and preserved on a stone inscription: it suggests that Gallio's year of office must have been either AD 51–52 or AD 52–53.

We can date Paul's eighteen-month stay in Corinth by this inscription from Delphi. It shows that Gallio, who was magistrate at the time of Paul's visit, came to Corinth as proconsul in AD 51 or 52.

Paul writes to the church at Thessalonica

At an early point in Paul's stay in Corinth, Silas and Timothy, who had stayed in Thessalonica, arrived with news of the church there. In the period of about six months since their conversion, the Thessalonian Christians had lived up to their responsibilities so well that the Christian message had been spread by their example through the whole of the surrounding area. But there were also some problems in the church. There had been attacks by the Jews, and maybe a more general persecution. There was

1 Thessalonians 1:1–10

1 Thessalonians 1:6

1 Thessalonians 4:3–8
1 Thessalonians 5:12–13

perhaps some sexual immorality, possibly a failure to respect the leaders of the church, and a curiosity about the state of Christians who died. So Paul wrote to encourage them in their difficulties and to give them direct guidance on their particular problems. His letter is preserved for us in the New Testament as 1 Thessalonians.

Above. This inscription, from one of Thessalonica's gates, mentions the rulers of the city as 'politarchs' – the term used in the account of Paul's visit in Acts. It helps reinforce the authenticity of the account in the Bible.

1 Thessalonians

After his usual introduction, Paul began by commending his readers for their faithfulness to the Christian message. Paul had told them how the risen and living Christ had revolutionized his own life, and he had challenged them with the fact that Christ could do the same for them by the power of the Holy Spirit. The Thessalonians had fully accepted this message, and the result had been that a strong church had been established. In addition, by the example of their changed lives, the Christian message had been commended to the pagan world around them. So much for the accusation flung against Paul in Galatia, that his message of freedom in Christ would lead to low moral standards! Quite the reverse had happened here, as the whole of Macedonia and Achaia saw the difference that the Christian faith made to the way of life of these believers (1 Thessalonians 1:2–10).

Paul and his converts

This, as Paul explains, was exactly what he and his helpers had hoped would happen. When they first visited Thessalonica with the Christian message they had been careful not to advertise themselves, but to draw attention to what they knew the risen Christ could do in the lives of the Thessalonians. Though they had been sent out on the authority of God himself, and with the approval of the Jewish churches, they followed the example of their Lord and Master, taking a low place as the servants of all men: 'we were gentle among you, like a nurse taking care of her children . . . we were ready to share with you not only the gospel of God but also our own selves' (2:7–8).

For this they had been well rewarded. The Thessalonians responded to the word of God. They recognized it as the means whereby men could enter into the full reality of life: 'when you received the word of God which you heard from us, you accepted it not as the word of men, but as what it really is, the word of God, which is at work in you believers'

(2:13). This, and the news brought by Silas and Timothy, proved a great encouragement to Paul as he worked in difficult conditions in Corinth (2:17–3:8).

Nevertheless, there was something lacking in their faith (3:10). So Paul set out to try to give good advice on the difficulties which Timothy had reported to him.

How should Christians behave?

One thing that often posed the greatest problem for converted pagans was the question of personal morality. In the pagan society of the day immorality of all kinds was normal. From what Paul says in chapter 1 of his letter, it is clear that the majority of the Thessalonian Christians had been enabled by the power of the Holy Spirit to overcome the pressure to be like their fellow citizens in this respect. But it was still necessary to reinforce what he had no doubt told them when he founded their church (4:1–8).

This was a subject that naturally led Paul to think of what he had written earlier in Galatians on the same matter: 'you were called to freedom . . . only do not use your freedom as an opportunity for the flesh, but through love be servants of one another' (Galatians 5:13). The Thessalonians had learnt this lesson well: 'you yourselves have been taught by God to love one another; and indeed you do love all the brethren throughout Macedonia' (1 Thessalonians 4:9–10).

It was a lesson that could never be over-emphasized. In a world in which the established order was rapidly changing, and in which men and women were frantically grasping at whatever religion came their way, one of the most important things the church could do was to display the love of Christ (4:9–12). Was not this what Jesus himself had taught? 'By this all men will know that you are my disciples, if you have love for one another' (John 13:35). The advice is here repeated and reinforced by Paul.

What about the future?

One thing above all was troubling the church at Thessalonica. They understood well the relationship that ought to exist among the members of their church. But what about those Christians who had died shortly after Paul's departure from the city? Paul found the answer to that in his conviction that the Lord he knew was present in the church by the operation of the Holy Spirit would one day come back openly and triumphantly (4:13–18). Meanwhile, the Thessalonian Christians should not worry unduly about loved ones who had died: 'since we believe that Jesus died and rose again, even so, through Jesus, God will bring with him those who have fallen asleep' (4:14).

Paul realized the possible trap in emphasizing what God would do in the future. So he went on to remind the Thessalonian Christians that their belief in the future return (or *parousia*) of Jesus was no excuse for inactivity in the present. Though some people would not be prepared for 'the day of the Lord', Christians ought to be. Their business was not to try and calculate 'the times and the seasons' (5:1), but to 'encourage one another and build one another up' (5:11).

Living the Christian life

Finally, Paul gave some advice to his readers on a number of topics, summarizing all that he had said before (5:12–21):

● In the church, the Christians should:
respect those who laboured among them – the elders whom Paul had presumably appointed in their church;
be at peace among themselves (a repetition and reinforcement of what he had said in 4:9–12);
encourage one another in their faith in Christ (5:14).

● In their everyday life, the Christians should:
return good for evil (5:15) – one of the most characteristic marks of the Christian (see also

Matthew 5:44);
'rejoice always' (5:16).

- In their individual relationship to God, the Christians must:
live in an attitude of prayer (5:17);
allow the Holy Spirit to direct their lives (5:19–20).

Paul signs off with his usual blessing and greeting, making a last appeal and promise to his readers. He knew that the secret of the Christian faith was the work of the living Lord operating in the lives of his followers. This was what he wanted them to keep in the forefront of their minds: 'He who calls you is faithful, and he will do it' (5:24).

But the Thessalonians were soon diverted away from the importance of God's faithfulness. They began instead to speculate on what Paul had said about the state of Christians who died, and the expected return (*parousia*) of Jesus. It was not long before Paul had to write another letter to help sort out the difficulties which, to some extent, the Thessalonian Christians seem to have invented for themselves out of certain parts of his first letter. Paul's second letter, known as 2 Thessalonians, is found alongside his first in our New Testament.

2 Thessalonians

In this second, shorter letter to the Thessalonians Paul clarifies three main points:

The church and its enemies

From what he says in 2 Thessalonians 1:5–12 it appears that the church had come under increasingly fierce persecution. This was to be expected; for the more widely known their love and Christian character became, the more could their enemies be expected to increase. The Jews and Romans never bothered about a religious faith that meant nothing to those holding it; but the revolutionary character of the life of the Thessalonian church naturally drew their attention to what was going on. It would be impossible to turn the world upside down without provoking some reaction from that world. Paul reminds these Christians that though for the moment things may be difficult, God is on their side. He will ultimately vindicate them.

The church and the future

A more subtle form of 'persecution' had also come into the church, with the appearance of letters claiming to be written by Paul and his associates (2 Thessalonians 2:1–12). Fanatics of some kind had taken advantage of Paul's mention of the *parousia* of Jesus in his earlier letter, and used the occasion to put their own point of view on the subject.

Paul had to warn the Thessalonian Christians 'not to be quickly shaken in mind or excited, either by spirit or by word, or by letter purporting to be from us, to the effect that the day of the Lord has come' (2:2). The precise meaning of the suggestion that 'the day of the Lord has come' is difficult to establish. In 1 Corinthians we find mention of people who thought that the resurrection (which was associated with the end of things, and the *parousia* of Christ) had already taken place. On the basis of this belief they indulged in all kinds of immoral practices (1 Corinthians 15:12–58). But it is difficult to connect the two groups of people in any direct way. In any event, Paul goes on to emphasize here that in his view the *parousia* of Jesus and all that it entails was not an event that could take place invisibly or mystically (which would need to be the case if it had already happened). On the contrary, he fixes his own hope firmly in history by making it clear that certain historical events connected with 'the man of lawlessness' (2:3–12), would herald the return of Christ.

The church and society

The outcome of the interest in future events that had arisen in Thessalonica was that some of the Christians had stopped living a normal life. They had opted out of society and were idly waiting for Christ to return, an attitude which Paul criticized severely. He regarded the Christian not as a man who shirked his duties by becoming a religious hermit, but as a man who played his full part in the society in which he lived. People who did not do this, however 'spiritual' their motive, should be

disciplined by the church. It was not very often that Paul instructed a church to take disciplinary action against one of its members, but this was one such case. Of course, the other Christians were to do this in a way that brought glory to the Lord whom they were serving: 'Do not look on him as an enemy, but warn him as a brother' (3:15).

Even with all their problems, however, the Thessalonian Christians had learned the true secret of the Christian way of life that Paul had shown them. They were rapidly becoming the kind of congregation of which Paul could be proud: 'your faith is growing abundantly, and the love of every one of you for one another is increasing' (1:3).

The Arch of Galerius, an impressive Roman structure, straddled the Egnatian Way at Thessalonica. Modern Thessaloniki is the second largest city of Greece.

It was in Thessalonica that Paul had been accused of 'turning the world upside down'. The congregation of Christians that he left behind him there continued this activity. As we read the letters Paul wrote to them, it is easy to conclude that the Thessalonian church was in serious difficulties. But we must not allow a few trivial criticisms to blind us to the fact that this is one of the very few congregations that Paul commends so warmly for their Christ-like character. The encouragement he received from this church must have been a great help to him as he faced the next big test of his life's work.

5 Paul the Pastor

Acts 18:18–21

WHEN Paul left Corinth he paid a short visit to Ephesus, and then returned direct to Caesarea in Palestine. From there he went straight to Antioch in Syria. After a short stay there he began what is often called his 'third missionary journey', which was not really a missionary expedition at all in the same way as his two earlier tours had been.

Acts 18:22

This third expedition was more in the nature of a pastor's ministry centred on two main places, Ephesus and Corinth. Paul began by a short trip through Galatia and Phrygia (the districts where he had been during his second expedition), but instead of going north to Troas, as before, he went direct to Ephesus.

Acts 18:22–19:1

Ephesus

Ancient Ephesus was an impressive city with baths, libraries, a theatre and market-place. The streets were paved with marble. At a lecture hall called the 'Hall of Tyrannus' Paul rented rooms to teach people his message. The harbour, long-since silted up, lies in the distance here.

Ephesus was the capital of the Roman province of Asia. It was a centre from which, by road or sea, Paul could easily keep in touch with most of the young churches he had already established in Asia Minor and in Europe. It was also a centre from which he and his colleagues could reach out into the whole province of Asia. His stay there resulted in churches being established in such places as Colossae and Laodicea, which Paul himself had not yet visited.

In the course of his three years' stay at Ephesus, Paul seems to have paid a short visit to Corinth. When he finally left Ephesus he went on to revisit the churches in Macedonia – probably

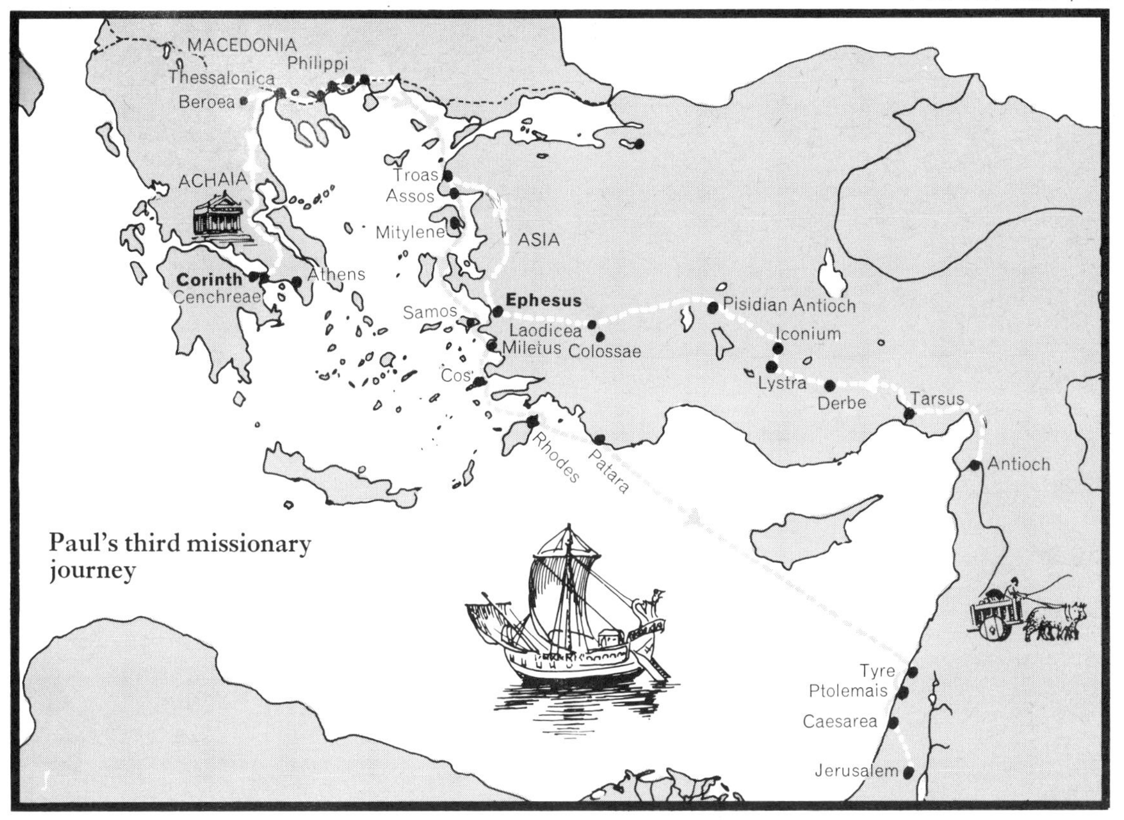

Paul's third missionary journey

Acts 20:1–2
Romans 15:19
Acts 20:3
Acts 20:4–6

Philippi, Thessalonica and Beroea. This may have been the occasion on which he went 'as far round as Illyricum', the region of Greece on the Dalmatian coast of the Adriatic Sea. For a further three months he stayed in Achaia (probably mostly in Corinth), then went back to Macedonia. There representatives of several churches, including Luke, joined him to take a gift from the Gentile congregations to the church in Jerusalem.

The impact of the gospel

Paul's long stay in Ephesus was undoubtedly the most important part of this period of his ministry – perhaps even the most important part of his whole life's work. Besides being the geographical centre of all the places Paul had previously visited, Ephesus was also a prominent centre of pagan religion. In it was to be found the great temple of Artemis (Diana) which was renowned as one of the wonders of the ancient world.

Acts 19:19
Acts 19:23–41

Paul's ministry in Ephesus was so successful that the two mainstays of Ephesian religious life were soon in danger of serious collapse. One of the things for which Ephesus was well known was its great number of magicians and sorcerers. Many of them became Christians and actually burnt their books of magic spells. The silversmiths of the city found that their trade in small replicas of the temple of Artemis for pilgrims began to decline, which led Demetrius and some others to start a riot against the Christians in the city.

Prison again?

1 Corinthians 15:32

In spite of such successes, however, Paul had great hardships at Ephesus – something he had come to expect when his ministry led to large-scale conversions to Christ. He states that he fought with wild beasts there, which may suggest he was thrown into the Roman arena, though it is probably a figure of speech. In 2 Corinthians 1:8 Paul speaks of the afflictions he endured in Asia; while in Romans 16:7, written probably just after he had left Ephesus, he writes of Andronicus and Junias as 'my fellow prisoners'. References such as these are often taken to indicate that Paul was imprisoned during this stay in Ephesus. The evidence for such an imprisonment is considered in more detail in chapter 7.

Paul the writer

This third period of Paul's ministry is of most interest to us because it is the period when three of Paul's greatest letters were written: 1 and 2 Corinthians and Romans. The fact that these letters later came to be accepted as Holy Scripture and admitted to a central place in the New Testament often tends to obscure for us the fact that they were originally real letters. They are not simply theological tracts written in the form of letters. Like Paul's earlier letters they follow the normal pattern of ancient letters, and each arose out of a specific historical situation.

After the riots protesting at Paul's teaching, the citizens of Ephesus gathered at the theatre, which could hold 25,000 people.

The Temple of Artemis (Diana) at Ephesus was four times the size of the Parthenon. This larger than life-sized Roman statue of the goddess is in white marble. It is based on the many-breasted mother-goddess figure of the earlier religion of this area.

Paul and the church at Corinth

Having said this, we have merely posed the problem and not solved it. The letters to Corinth in particular confront us with one of the most complicated historical puzzles of the entire New Testament. Galatians and 1 and 2 Thessalonians were fairly easy to fit into the picture of Paul's activities recorded in Acts. But in the case of 1 and 2 Corinthians we have no information at all from Acts. In order to piece together the historical situation behind this correspondence we depend entirely on the vague hints and allusions which Paul made as he wrote. It was not his main purpose to give a historical account of his own movements or of the state of the Corinthian church, so any reconstruction of what was going on must be more or less imaginative. But there is general agreement among most scholars that Paul's dealings with the church in Corinth at this time can be summarized in six stages:

Bad news from Corinth

During his three years' stay at Ephesus, Paul received bad news of the state of the Corinth church. So he wrote a letter warning them of the dangers of immorality. This is the letter referred to in 1 Corinthians 5:11, where Paul says: 'I wrote to you not to associate with any one who bears the name of brother if he is guilty of immorality . . .'. Some scholars think that part of this letter could be preserved in what we now call 2 Corinthians – in 6:14–7:1 – since this section seems to be out of character with

Opposite. The great Temple of Artemis lay 1½ miles outside Ephesus. Today it is merely a great rectangular swamp, littered with broken columns.

its context in 2 Corinthians, and it begins 'Do not be mismated with unbelievers . . .'.

Paul writes 1 Corinthians

Members of Chloe's household also brought reports that the Corinthian church was dividing into different parties. Paul's own authority as an apostle was being challenged (1 Corinthians 1:11). These reports had later been confirmed by Stephanas and two others (1 Corinthians 16:17) who brought with them a letter from Corinth asking certain definite questions. 1 Corinthians was probably Paul's reply to this letter.

Paul visits Corinth

After this, Paul learned, perhaps from Timothy who had returned from Corinth to Ephesus, that his letter was having no effect. At this point he decided to pay a short visit to Corinth to see for himself what was happening. No such visit is mentioned in Acts, but it is certainly implied in 2 Corinthians 2:1; 12:14 and 13:1. On this visit he must have come, as he had threatened in 1 Corinthians 4:21, 'with a rod', for it could be called a 'painful visit' (2 Corinthians 2:1).

Another letter

After his return to Ephesus Paul sent Titus with a much stronger letter, written 'out of much affliction and anguish of heart', as he tells us in 2 Corinthians 2:4. Some think this letter is now preserved in our 2 Corinthians chapters 10–13, where Paul vigorously dismisses attacks made on his apostolic authority, which was almost certainly the subject of this third letter.

Good news from Corinth

Paul then left for Macedonia, having been driven away from Ephesus (Acts 20:1). In Macedonia he met Titus again, who brought welcome news of a change of attitude in the Corinthian church. He also carried an invitation for Paul to go to Corinth (2 Corinthians 7:5–16).

Paul writes 2 Corinthians

Paul sent back to Corinth with Titus a more compassionate letter, expressing his great joy. This letter is probably what we now know as 2 Corinthians chapters 1–9. He also took this opportunity to write on other subjects: the relation of preachers and hearers; the hope of a life after death; the general theme of salvation; and the collection which he was organizing for the Jerusalem church. If 2 Corinthians 10–13 belongs to this same letter, Paul must have heard news of a further revolt against his authority at Corinth while he was actually writing to them, which led him to defend his own position as an accredited apostle of Christ. Some scholars think that 2 Corinthians 10–13, rather than being earlier than 2 Corinthians 1–9 or written at the same time, was actually a letter sent later, when Paul's authority was again being undermined.

So much for the 'mechanics' of how these letters came to be written. But what was Paul actually saying to these Christians? In trying to answer that question, it will be best for us to pick out certain features of what Paul said, from which we can gain a picture of the situation in the church at Corinth. It is in **1 Corinthians** that we find most information about this situation. Paul's argument there falls conveniently into three sections, which may be given the titles: **Life in Christ**; **Life in the World**; and **Life in the Church**.

1 Corinthians

Life in Christ
(1 Corinthians 1:10–4:21)

One of the things that characterized the city of Corinth was the varied nature of its society. Its position as an important sea port on one of the busiest routes in the Mediterranean ensured this. In the streets of Corinth military men from Rome, mystics from the east and Jews from Palestine continually rubbed shoulders with the philosophers of Greece. When Paul had preached the good news about Jesus in this city, it was a cross-section of this cosmopolitan society that responded and formed the Christian church in Corinth.

Not surprisingly, men and women from such different spiritual and intellectual backgrounds brought with them into the church some very different concepts and ideas. While Paul was with them the various sections of the young congregation were held together. But on his departure these new Christians began to work out for themselves the implications of their Christian faith, and naturally began to produce different answers.

A divided church. As a result the church at Corinth had for all practical purposes been divided into four different groups, of which Paul speaks in 1 Corinthians 1:10–17. Some were claiming that their spiritual allegiance was to Paul, others to Apollos, others to Cephas, while yet others claimed only to belong to Christ (1:12–13). These four parties clearly reflect the diverse backgrounds of the Corinthian Christians:

- The 'Paul Party' would consist of libertines. They were people who had heard Paul's original preaching on the freedom of the Christian and concluded from it that, once they had responded to the Christian gospel, they could live as they liked. This was exactly what the Judaizers who opposed Paul in Galatia had said would happen when the Christian message was declared without making people obey the Old Testament Law. Paul in fact always emphasized that, far from relieving Christians of moral obligations, his message actually made deeper demands on them. But this danger of lawlessness ('antinomianism') was always present in his churches.
- The 'Cephas Party' were undoubtedly legalists. They were people like the Judaizers in Jerusalem, who believed that the Christian life meant the strict observance of the Jewish Law, both ritual and moral. Many of them had probably been Jews or Gentile 'God-fearers' before they were converted to the Christian faith.
- The 'Apollos Party' were probably devotees of the classical Greek outlook. Apollos is mentioned in Acts 18:24–28, where we learn that he was a Jew from Alexandria, 'an eloquent man, well versed in the scriptures'. Alexandria in Egypt had a large Jewish population, and several influential and gifted teachers lived and worked there both before and after the New Testament period. Best known among these was Philo (about 20 BC–AD 45), a Jew who specialized in interpreting the Old Testament in accordance with the concepts of Greek philosophy. He was trying to show that all that was in the Greek philosophers had actually been foreshadowed by Moses and other Old Testament writers. As an educated Alexandrian Jew, Apollos would be steeped in this kind of scriptural interpretation. He would naturally be an acceptable teacher to those Christians at Corinth with a Greek philosophical background.
- The 'Christ Party' probably consisted of a group of men and women who considered themselves to be above the groups that had developed around the personalities of ordinary men. They wanted a direct contact with Christ himself, in the same way as they had experienced direct mystical contacts with gods in the pagan eastern Mystery Religions. If Serapis could be called 'lord', so could Christ. But Paul made it

clear to them that in fact, 'no one can say "Jesus is Lord" except by the Holy Spirit' (1 Corinthians 12:3). What they were trying to do was to exchange one mystery god for another. Since this kind of belief often led to libertinism in practice, these people may well have found themselves siding with the 'Paul Party' on some important ethical issues.

The confusion at Corinth. As we read through 1 Corinthians we can see how each of these groups was at work, spreading its own ideas and emphases. *The libertines*, who claimed to follow Paul, encouraged the whole church not to worry about open immorality (5:1–13). *The legalists*, claiming to follow Cephas' example, raised the old question of what kind of food Christians should eat. But this time the argument was over food that had been offered in pagan temples before being sold to the public (chapters 8–9). *The philosophers*, followers of Apollos, were insisting that they had a form of wisdom that was superior to anything Paul had proclaimed (1:18–25). *The mystics*, claiming they were following Christ, were inclined to argue that the sacraments of the church acted in a supernatural way. They claimed they did not have to worry about the natural results of their immoral activities (10:1–13). The resurrection had already come, they claimed, for they had been raised in a mystical way with Christ (15:12–19). They claimed they were now living on a super-spiritual level of existence, far beyond the grasp of the followers of Paul, Cephas or Apollos (see also 4:8).

The combination of these different types of extremism led in the second century to the formation of a heretical movement known as 'Gnosticism'. We can probably see here in Corinth the first stirrings in this direction. But at the time, Paul was not concerned with giving a name to this movement. All he saw was one of his largest churches thrown into utter confusion by fanatics operating from four different directions.

This was totally against all that he understood the Christian message to be. He had told the Galatians that belief in Christ created a new fellowship of equality and freedom for all Christians, something that he had himself experienced as he moved from city to city and found new friends among the unlikeliest of people simply because they had been united in Christ.

The answer in Christ. He knew therefore that the answer to the Corinthian situation must be found in Christ. Neither Paul himself, nor Cephas, nor Apollos, nor the kind of 'Christ' that was being followed in Corinth, could achieve any lasting result. When he first visited Corinth Paul had declared the cross of Christ and his resurrection to be 'of first importance' in the understanding of the Christian faith (1 Corinthians 15:3–7; 1:18–25). This was the only basis on which men and women of diverse cultures could be reunited. Whatever Paul, Apollos or Cephas had done in their own name was of no consequence. So Paul repeated his basic message as the answer to the problems of the Corinthian church: 'No other foundation can anyone lay than that which is laid, which is Jesus Christ' (3:11).

Having set out his own starting-point, Paul went on to look at some of the specific problems of the church at Corinth; problems concerned with their attitudes to non-Christian standards and institutions, and with their attitudes to one another in the gatherings of the church.

Life in the world
(1 Corinthians 5:1–11:1)

Though Christians enjoyed new privileges by virtue of their new life in Christ, they still had to live in a non-Christian world. In Corinth, three main areas posed problems concerning the Christian's relationships with non-Christians:

Christian behaviour. At least two of the 'parties' in the Corinth church claimed to have a theological reason for ignoring the accepted Christian standards of morality. In the central part of his letter Paul mentions three specific matters which had come to his attention.

● Permissiveness. One thing that particularly worried him was the report that 'there is immorality among you . . . of a kind that is not found even among pagans; for a man is living with his father's wife' (5:1). Paul was never one for taking drastic action against people with whom he disagreed. But this kind of behaviour was so serious that he felt he had no alternative but to instruct the church members not to associate with the person concerned until he had repented of his sin. He told them: 'When you are assembled, and my spirit is present, with the power of our Lord Jesus, you are to deliver this man to Satan for the destruction of the flesh, that his spirit may be saved in the day of the Lord Jesus' (5:4–5). Some parts of this instruction are difficult for us to understand. But the main point is clear: this kind of sin was so serious that it must be completely destroyed. The person concerned must leave the Christian fellowship – though his final spiritual fate is not the business of the local church but will be revealed 'in the day of the Lord Jesus'.

● Freedom. Once again Paul had to emphasize that freedom in Christ does not mean the freedom to be immoral (6:12–20). Christians are not free to do as they please, but free to serve God, to whom they belong (6:19–20).

● Marriage. One of the questions which the Corinthians had asked Paul was also concerned with marriage and divorce (7:1–40). In replying Paul permits Christians to marry (7:1–9), though he himself was not married and he could 'wish that all were as I myself am' (7:7). He forbids divorce (7:10–11), except in a case where a heathen partner deserts a Christian (7:12–16). And he recommends that the Corinthian Christians should remain in their present condition, either married or single (7:17–24), though he recommends celibacy as the preferable state (7:25–40).

This was clearly advice given for a specific situation that had arisen in Corinth. It is interesting to note the way Paul separates his own advice and opinion from what he believed to be the will of his Master. He felt that he had Jesus' authority for saying there should be no divorce among Christians (7:10–11). But on the other issues with which he deals, in one case he makes it plain that it is 'not the Lord' who is speaking (7:12), and in another he merely says, 'I think that I have the Spirit of God' (7:40).

Some of the things Paul says seem odd to us, to put it mildly. Scholars down the ages have made various suggestions as to why Paul should appear to run down the institution of marriage here. No doubt he had been jilted when young, they tell us, or even perhaps unhappily married! But such explanations fail to take account of the historical context in which he wrote these things. He was aware that the situation of the Corinthian church was extremely serious (7:26), and there were many more important things to be done than making arrangements for weddings.

Was it not something like this that Jesus himself had said? 'If any one comes to me and does not hate his own father and mother and wife and children and brothers and sisters, yes, and even his own life, he cannot be my disciple' (Luke 14:26). There is a striking similarity between this and what Paul says (7:29–31). Yet no one seriously suggests that Jesus was against marriage and family life. Quite the opposite; for it is widely supposed that he raised the whole issue to a much higher level. Examination of the other passages in Paul's writings where he treats the same subject will show that he held marriage in the same high regard as Jesus did (see Ephesians

5:22–33). In 1 Corinthians he was addressing himself to Christians in a desperate situation, and in such a case drastic action was called for.

Christians and the civil law. Another thing that concerned Paul was the way Christians in Corinth were quarrelling with each other, and then going to the civil law courts to sort out their grievances. Paul had to condemn this practice out of hand. For one thing, it was quite absurd that Christians, who claimed to be brothers and sisters, should go to pagan courts at all. When a quarrel arises in a family, it should not be necessary to go to court with it. Surely some member of the church fellowship was wise enough to sort the problem out (6:1–6).

But what disturbed Paul more was that quarrels should arise at all. Christians ought to follow the example set to them by Christ, and 'suffer wrong' rather than create division in the Christian fellowship (6:7–8). In the light of what God has done for them in Christ, their petty bickerings fade into insignificance (6:9–11).

Everyday life. It was possible for Christians to live independently of the pagan courts. But they could not help getting involved in other aspects of pagan life in a city like Corinth. Take, for example, the question of food. In our modern world, if we want meat we go to the shop and buy it. Unless we are vegetarians, there are no moral problems involved.

But in Corinth there were no butcher's shops. The purchase of meat was a religious activity. The only meat available for sale was from the carcasses of the animals offered in sacrifice at the various pagan temples. Other meat may have been available in the Jewish community of a Roman city, but that was no help to Christians. They did not want to conform to the Jewish food regulations, nor did Jews want to supply Christians with meat.

So the only alternative appeared to be to buy meat that had been offered to pagan gods, which the Christians knew did not really exist anyway. But this was just the problem. For some of the church members felt that by buying meat of this kind they were somehow encouraging and sharing in the worship of pagan gods. What then was the Christian to do? Paul takes up the matter in 1 Corinthians 8:1–11:1, where he makes the following four points:

- The Christian is free to eat food that had been offered to pagan gods, since such gods do not exist. But the Christian who understands this must also have a brotherly concern for those who see the matter differently. So the 'enlightened' Christian should occasionally be prepared to forgo the freedom to eat food bought from the pagan temples out of consideration for other people (8:1–13).
- This was the kind of concession that Paul himself had made, in a different sphere. As God's messenger Paul had the right to be supported by God's people: 'the Lord commanded that those who proclaim the gospel should get their living by the gospel' (9:14). Paul had given up his right to be maintained in this way, and instead practised self-discipline (9:1–27). He had been willing to place himself under restrictions so that his message might be accepted by all kinds of men: 'though I am free from all men, I have made myself a slave to all, that I might win the more' (9:19).
- Christians should also recognize that there could be real dangers in participating in heathen festivals (10:1–22). Some of the Corinthian Christians had the idea that the Christian sacraments gave them a sort of magical immunity from pagan rituals, so that they could take part without being truly spiritually involved. Paul points out from the history of Israel that this was not so. It was quite impossible to share in the Lord's Supper one day and a

heathen feast the next and escape without harm.

● The general principle to be followed in reaching practical decisions on these ethical questions is not to do anything that would lead others astray, even things that are right in themselves, but to 'do all to the glory of God' (10:23–11:1).

Life in the church
(1 Corinthians 11:2–15:58)

Paul had been asked the answer to several specific questions that were puzzling the church at Corinth. Some of them we have already considered, questions concerning marriage and divorce, and food bought from pagan temples. But there were others, concerned with the church's worship (11:2–14:40) and beliefs (15:1–58).

The church's worship (11:2–14:40). As the church at Corinth met for worship, trying to put into practice what Paul had taught them, three practical difficulties had arisen:

● Freedom in worship. Paul had taught the Christians at Corinth the same things as he had taught the churches of Galatia. Two of the basic points of this message had been that in Christ there is to be no distinction of race, class or sex (Galatians 3:28); and that Christ has given Christians a new freedom (Galatians 5:1). In practical terms of the church's worship, this meant that Paul, contrary to the Jewish custom of the day, allowed women to play a full part in the Christian ministry. He had passed on 'traditions' to that effect to the Corinthian church (1 Corinthians 11:2), traditions which the church members had observed. But they misunderstood the character of Christian freedom. Women who were taking a leading part in the church's services were doing in God's presence things they would not have done in front of their neighbours.

The prevailing social custom of the time laid down that respectable, modest women did not appear in public with their heads uncovered. The Corinthian Christians, however, argued that the Christian was set free even from the normal rules of society, and was able to express this freedom before God in the church. Paul could see that this was a similar situation to the one which had arisen in the church over food bought in pagan temples. But in this case the women in the church were offending the non-Christian society which they were trying to evangelize. So he suggested that women taking a public part in the church's worship ought to follow the prevailing social custom and do so with their heads veiled (11:2–16).

What Paul said about women in the letter to Corinth

If 1 Corinthians 11:2–16 was all that Paul said about women, there would be no real problem in understanding his thought on the matter. But what he says in 1 Corinthians 14:33b–35 appears to forbid the very thing that he had allowed, indeed encouraged, in 11:2–16. What concerned Paul in 11:2–16 was that women were taking an active part in the church services without conforming to the social conventions of the day. He does not insist on the veiling of those women who were present in church but did not take a leading part. In 14:33b–35, on the other hand, he says: 'the women should keep silence in the churches. For they are not permitted to speak . . .' (14:34). This has caused many problems for interpreters. The following points need to be considered:

● Paul's teaching on freedom in Christ and the unity that exists between people related by a mutual fellowship with Christ directly contradicts what he says about women keeping silent in church in 14:33b–35.

● If 1 Corinthians 14:33b–35 is a genuine part of the text (see below), it must be explained in terms of what was going on in Corinth, and not as a general principle. If it is taken as a general principle, we would need to suppose that Paul was consciously contradicting what he had written in 11:2–16 which, with its appeal to creation, has at least the appearance of being a general principle. Such an approach lands us in absurdity. For an intelligent man like Paul would hardly state two contradictory principles without any further explanation. But he may well have stated a general principle and then given slightly different advice to deal with a specific situation.

● If, as we have suggested, there was something like what later came to be known as 'Gnostic' teaching in the background of 1 Corinthians, this can provide us with a possible clue to the interpretation of 1 Corinthians 11:2–16 and 14:33b–35. The only other New Testament book which contains instructions similar to 14:33b–35 was certainly written to oppose Gnostic tendencies (1 Timothy 2:8–15). In the Gnostic heresies of the second century certain women played a large and conspicuous part. This was one reason why the church after the New Testament period officially excluded women from any form of public service.

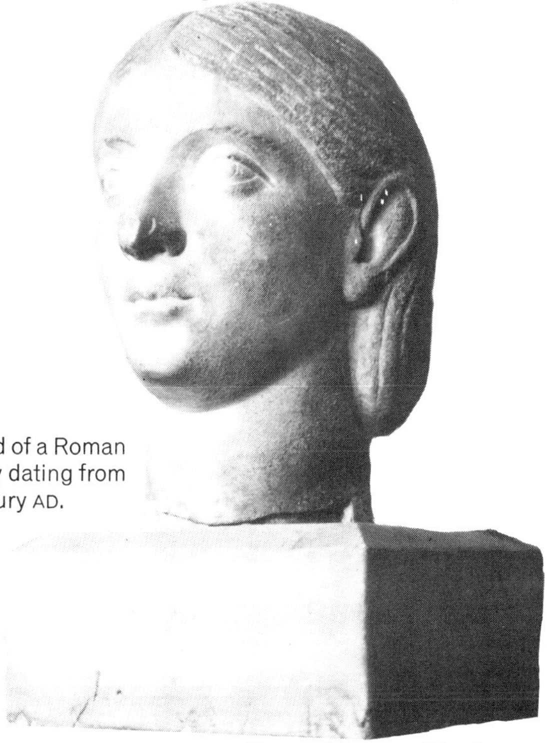

The stylized head of a Roman woman, probably dating from the second century AD.

● There is a certain amount of evidence in the ancient manuscripts of our New Testament to suggest that 1 Corinthians 14:33b–35 may not be part of what Paul originally wrote. It could have been added later at a time when Gnostic women were being opposed in the church at large.

Probably the best explanation is to treat these verses as being a part of what Paul originally wrote. For the oldest and best manuscripts of the New Testament include them. In this case we must explain their distinctive emphasis by some historical facts. The freedom to take a public part in the worship of the church, which Paul allows in 11:2–16, is obviously in line with his own teaching on equality and freedom in Christ, and the rules which he lays down to limit this freedom can easily be explained on the principle of being 'all things to all men' (1 Corinthians 9:22). But in the situation as he knew it at Corinth, he perhaps felt, on second thoughts, that it would be better if the particular women concerned there took no part at all. This point of view is all the more reasonable if we believe that they were connected with some form of Gnostic heresy. It is also perhaps worth noting that what Paul says in 14:33b–35 could only apply to married women, and not to unmarried ones. This is another indication that it was a specific group of people whom Paul had in mind here.

So Paul allowed the two contradictory statements to stand; one as a declaration of his basic principles (11:2–16), and the other as a specific piece of advice for the church in Corinth (14:33b–35).

● Morals and worship. The way the church was observing the Lord's Supper (communion) also gave cause for concern (11:17–34). Instead of carrying out the instructions which Jesus himself gave, and which Paul had delivered to them at an earlier stage (11:23–26), the Corinthian Christians were making the service into an occasion for feasting and merriment. They were all bringing along their own food, and having private feasts – feasts which they ought to have held in their own homes (11:22).

The party divisions that Paul was so much against were rearing their ugly heads even at the Lord's table (11:18–19). All this division, and the accompanying revelry and drunkenness in the church, was dishonouring both to the purpose of their gathering and also to the Christians themselves. They were giving no thought to what they were doing, and some of them had brought upon themselves the judgement which they deserved (11:29–32).

● Gifts and worship. Another very important feature in the Corinthian church was the exercise of spiritual gifts.

Basic to Christian experience in the apostolic churches was the conviction that a Christian was a person who possessed the Holy Spirit. He was a 'charismatic', a person who possessed *charismata*, or spiritual gifts: speaking in ecstatic tongues (glossolalia), interpretation of such tongues, prophecy (as in Acts 13:1–2), and the working of miracles by the apostles (Acts 19:11–12).

The Corinthian church possessed all of these gifts and many more in abundance, and they were so eager to exercise them that several people could be taking part in church worship at the same time. This was clearly an unsatisfactory way of going on. Paul had to remind them that 'God is not a God of confusion but of peace' (1 Corinthians 14:33). This meant that when the gifts were exercised in the church, it could be taken for granted that if God was truly inspiring them, they would occur in a way that would lead to the building up of the whole church (12:7).

Paul recognized the validity of all the gifts that had appeared in Corinth. He emphasized that every one of them was God-given and therefore had its rightful place in gatherings of the congregation. Just as the human body has different parts, each of which must make its contribution to the smooth operation of the body, so it is in the church. Each of the gifts possessed by different members of the church should contribute to the smooth running of the whole (12:14–31).

Not every Christian would be given one of the more spectacular gifts, such as tongues, but all had their part to play. One gift should be common to all: the gift of love. Love, for fellow-Christians and fellow-men in general, was the basis on which Christians ought to desire and seek after the other gifts (14:1–2).

The church's belief (15:1–58). Finally, Paul deals with what he regarded as the core of essential Christian belief. It was also one of the main elements in the problems of the Corinthian church: the resurrection of Christ.

Some members of the church were claiming that in their mystical experiences they had already been raised to a new spiritual level above that achieved by the more ordinary church members. This belief was linked with a misunderstanding about the resurrection of Jesus, and Paul deals with it in two ways.

First he reminds the Corinthians of the firm historical foundation on which belief in the resurrection of Jesus is based (15:3–11). In doing this he gives us the earliest account in the New Testament of the resurrection of Jesus. Secondly he goes on to show how, if the resurrection of Jesus happened historically (as he and the other apostles believed it did), this must be a guarantee that Christians also will be raised at the last day in the same way as Jesus was raised from the dead. Because of the centrality of Jesus' resurrection for the whole of Christian belief, anyone who denied this by spiritualizing it into mystical experiences was in fact denying the basis of the Christian faith: 'if the dead are not raised, then Christ has not been raised. If Christ has not been raised, your faith is futile and you are still in your sins . . . we are of all men most to be pitied' (15:16–18).

Prominent among the ruins of ancient Corinth is the Temple of Apollo, behind which rises the rock of Acrocorinth.

So Paul came to the end of what must be the most complicated letter he ever wrote. Like Galatians, it was written in the white heat of controversy, which only adds to our difficulties in understanding it. Paul was under attack by his friends as well as his enemies. This must have given him considerable reason to pause and think out his gospel again. He wanted to avoid the pitfalls of the past without in any sense compromising his basic position that in Christ all barriers of race, sex and social standing are removed, and all men and women stand equal in the freedom given to them by the Holy Spirit. It was probably thoughts of this kind that dictated the form of Paul's next major letter, which is quite different from any of those we have looked at so far.

Some of the Christians at Corinth had scruples about eating the meat available, since it had been offered at pagan temples. This inscription is from the meat market (*macellum*) in Corinth.

Paul's goal

Rome was naturally Paul's ultimate goal in spreading the good news about Jesus throughout the empire. But Rome had already been evangelized, and had a flourishing church. Many of the Christians in Rome were probably of Jewish origin, and Paul realized that some of them may have been influenced against him. Christians from Judea may well have been there saying it was necessary for all Gentile converts to observe the Law of the Old Testament. If they had heard of what was happening in Corinth they could have been confirmed in their false impression of his message.

Paul visits Corinth

Acts 20:2–3
Romans 15:25–27
Romans 1:11
Romans 15:24

Towards the end of his dealings with the Corinthian church, Paul visited the area of Corinth, and spent some three months there. After this he intended to go to Jerusalem with delegates from the Gentile churches who were taking a gift to the Jewish church. Later he hoped to visit Rome and then go on into Spain.

Rome was of crucial importance in the evangelization of the empire. And there was also the need to re-state his own gospel in a form that was not open to misinterpretation, either by sympathisers or by opponents. So Paul decided to prepare for his visit to the capital by writing a letter to the church there, containing a complete statement of his own beliefs. This was the letter to the Romans.

Romans

How Christians know God

The first part of Romans, chapters 1–8, is one long theological argument starting from a text in the prophet Habakkuk: 'the just shall live by faith' (Habakkuk 2:4). Here Paul argues in a way very familiar to us from Galatians; indeed many of the points he makes are the same. All men, both Jews and Gentiles, are under the power of sin. Apart from Christ they have no way of escape from God's condemnation of sin (1:18–3:20). Yet it is possible for men to receive 'the righteousness of God', that is, release from God's sentence of condemnation and the power to share in God's own goodness. This is something that can be obtained only through faith in Christ, and not by good works (3:21–4:25).

As in Galatians, Paul illustrates his theme from the life of Abraham (4:1–25). He then goes on (5:1–8:39) to describe the results of this new relationship with God: freedom from the wrath of God; freedom from slavery to sin; freedom from the Law; and freedom from death through the working of the Spirit of God in Christ. 'In all these things we are more than conquerors through him who loved us' (8:37).

These are all themes that Paul had dealt with before in either Galatians or 1 Corinthians. But here we find several new elements. They are all clearly a result of Paul's experience as he had seen his message misunderstood and misapplied in the churches. Paul deals directly with the problem of antinomianism in 6:1–8:39. He makes it clear that though Christians are set free from the rule of all external law for gaining an acceptable standing before God, they have in fact entered into a new kind of service. No longer are they 'slaves of sin' (6:17); they are now 'slaves of God' (6:22). Christians have been set free not to do as they please, but that by the work of the Holy Spirit within them they might be 'conformed to the image of his Son' (8:29). This is the teaching of Galatians as seen by Paul after his experiences in Corinth.

Israel and salvation

In chapters 9–11 Paul moves on. He is concerned with the fact of Israel's rejection of this salvation which he has been describing. He points out that God's apparent rejection of the Jews does not contradict either his promises in the Old Testament or his justice. It is Israel's own fault. She chose the way of 'works' rather than the way of faith. But Paul was still convinced that God's rejection of Israel was not final. Even in the midst of such unfaithfulness, there was a faithful remnant (11:1–10). The present rejection of the Jews was in fact fully part of God's plan for the ultimate salvation of people from all races (11:11–36).

How Christians should behave

Paul then moves away from strictly theological statements to write about the practical application of God's righteousness in Christian living (12:1–15:13). Here he deals with the Christian's relationship to the church (12:1–8), to other people (12:9–21) and to the state (13:1–10). He sums up Christian duty as a whole in the words 'love is the fulfilling of the Law' (13:10). He emphasizes again that standards of Christian morality are to be produced not by an artificial set of rules and regulations imposed from outside, but by the power of the Holy Spirit working within the believer. But the end result of the Spirit's work will be that the Law of God is in fact observed, and the key idea of this law is love. Paul illustrates this by reference to two live issues: the eating of vegetables in preference to meat (14:1–15:6; a similar case to the question of meat bought from pagan temples), and the general attitude of Jews and Gentiles towards one another within the church (15:7–13).

In this letter we have a mature statement of the gospel as Paul understood it. It was a gospel that did not depend on keeping rules and regulations. It was rather a revolutionary message, the message of the living Lord who wanted to be in control of the lives of his followers. Under his direction they would discover a way of living that would be pleasing to God and beneficial to their fellow-men. This was something that no one liked, whether Jew or Gentile. But all the same Paul was convinced that it was 'the power of God for salvation'. It was obtained through faith in Christ. But the Christian faith also demanded submission to Christ as Lord, and openness to the power of the Holy Spirit working in the believer's life.

Romans 1:16

6 Paul reaches Rome

Romans 15:23

At the end of his letter to the Roman church, Paul made the extraordinary statement: 'I no longer have any room for work in these regions.' Yet we know it would be quite foolish to suppose that by this time the whole of Asia Minor and the Balkan peninsula, where Paul had been working, had been evangelized with the Christian message.

Paul's missionary strategy

But Paul viewed his own missionary task in a slightly different way. He saw his job to be the formation of Christian congregations at strategic points throughout the Roman Empire. From these the surrounding regions could be reached. At this point in his ministry he had completed that kind of work in the areas where he had been operating. He had founded thriving and growing churches in all the main centres of population. The business of establishing other churches in the surrounding areas was now the responsibility of the new Christian converts.

Paul had his sights set on a higher goal. His own special responsibility was to ensure that during the course of his lifetime the gospel would be spread throughout the whole civilized world, which for him meant the Roman Empire. Italy already had churches at its most important centres, including Rome, and so Paul saw Spain as his next objective. Yet at the same time he believed that, as the 'apostle to the Gentiles', he had something to contribute to the church in the most strategic position of all: Rome the capital of the empire. Even though he was normally reluctant to enter what had previously been the sphere of other missionaries, one of his main ambitions was to visit the city of Rome. But before this, he had other problems to face.

Paul and his own people

Romans 15:31

Acts 21:20–21

In writing to the Roman Christians Paul had made what seems to have been almost a prophetic statement. He asked them to pray for him, 'that I may be delivered from the unbelievers in Judea, and that my service for Jerusalem may be acceptable to the saints'. Paul was hated in Judea more than anywhere else, even by some of those who called themselves Christians. In their eyes, he was nothing less than a traitor to the Jewish faith. As a Pharisee he had been entrusted with the priceless privilege of interpreting the Old Testament Law. As a Christian, they said, he had despised his privilege, declaring the Law to be inadequate as a means of salvation, and powerless as a source of moral inspiration.

This was something that troubled Paul very much. Contrary to what his opponents thought, he held his own Jewish heritage to be very valuable. He was reluctant to think that God had altogether rejected the Jewish people. He believed that they had misunderstood the whole point of the Old Testament while he, Paul, now saw its full meaning because of his new relationship with Jesus Christ, who was its true fulfilment.

As a sign of his own continuing care for his people, Paul had organized in the Gentile congregations a collection for the Jewish church at Jerusalem. Surely this would show that, whatever theological differences might exist between the Jewish and Gentile Christian churches, they were united in a practical way.

Back to Jerusalem

Acts 20:4–6

Paul set off for Jerusalem in the company of Christians from Beroea, Thessalonica, Derbe and Ephesus, along with Luke and Timothy. He must have known that in some ways he was taking a foolhardy step, for on the journey he stopped off at Miletus and

sent for the elders of the Ephesian church. In the course of his talk with them he made it clear that he did not expect to see them again. He knew that all he could expect at the hands of the Jews was 'imprisonment and afflictions'. But, as on previous occasions, he put the glory of his Lord and Master before his own safety: 'I do not account my life of any value nor as precious to myself, if only I may accomplish my course and the ministry which I received from the Lord Jesus, to testify to the gospel of the grace of God.'

Acts 20:23

Acts 20:24

When he arrived in Jerusalem, Paul's fears and expectations were fully realized. Reports brought to Judea by foreign Jews had contained exaggerated accounts of Paul's break with Judaism. They made no mention of those concessions Paul had sometimes made to Jewish prejudices. James, who was now the leader of the church in Jerusalem, explained the situation to him more fully: 'You see, brother, how many thousands there are among the Jews of those who have believed; they are all zealous for the law, and they have been told about you that you teach all the Jews who are among the Gentiles to forsake Moses, telling them not to circumcise their children or observe the customs.'

Acts 21:20–21

Above. Erastus, City Treasurer in Corinth, sent his greetings to fellow-Christians in Rome, at the end of Paul's letter (Romans 16:23). He is probably the same man as is named in this inscription from Corinth: 'Erastus laid this pavement at his own expense, in appreciation of his appointment as *aedile*.'

'All things to all men'

Acts 21:23–24

1 Corinthians 9:22

James, like Paul himself, hoped the collection brought by Paul and his friends would pacify these hostile Jewish Christians. He also advised Paul to make a peace gesture to the Jews themselves, by paying the expenses involved in a ritual vow taken by four Jewish Christians, and by sharing in their fast. Paul agreed to do this. His policy had always been one of fitting in with all kinds of men: 'I have become all things to all men, that I might by all means save some.'

Acts 21:27–29

Towards the end of this fast, some Jews from the province of Asia spotted Paul in the Temple. They worked themselves up into believing that he had defiled the Temple by taking some of his Gentile companions into its inner court.

To do this was a very serious crime. It was one of the very few crimes carrying the death penalty that the Romans allowed the Jews to try and punish themselves. To ensure that no one committed this crime unknowingly, an inscription stood over the main gate of the Temple in Paul's day. It read, in three languages: 'No foreigner may enter within the barricade which surrounds the Temple and its enclosure. Anyone who is caught doing so will have himself to blame for his ensuing death.' Two such inscriptions, in Greek, have been found by archaeologists on the Temple site in Jerusalem.

Prisoner in Jerusalem

Acts 21:30–36

Acts 22:22–29

The Jews who saw Paul in the Temple wanted to act without the decision of a court by killing him there and then. But the Roman commander arrived and rescued Paul – not because of any sympathy for the apostle, but probably in the hope of avoiding a riot. This Roman commander assumed that Paul must be some sort of political agitator. He was about to have him flogged to get the truth from him when Paul claimed the immunity from such treatment which was his right as a Roman citizen.

Acts 23:1–10

The next step was to call a meeting of the Jewish supreme council, the Sanhedrin. The accusation against Paul was clearly a religious matter concerned with the Jewish Law, and the Sanhedrin was the proper body to deal with such a question. But the meeting ended in uproar when Paul started a quarrel between the Pharisees and Sadducees by stating that he was still a good Pharisee and believed in the resurrection of the dead.

Tried before Felix

Acts 23:12–24

Jerusalem had always been a dangerous place for the Romans. When it was learned that a plan was afoot to kill Paul he was taken under strong guard to Caesarea, the Roman headquarters on the coast of Palestine. There he would escape the direct notice of the Jewish authorities.

At Caesarea Paul was again tried before the Roman procurator Felix. This time the charge was not only that of defiling the Temple, but also of provoking civil disorder wherever he went. There is a clear parallel here between the trials of Paul and the

Anyone could enter the outer court of the Temple in Jerusalem; but Gentiles were forbidden to enter the inner courts on pain of death. Inscriptions in Greek (like this one) and Latin warned visitors of this penalty.

Paul was kept prisoner for two years at Caesarea, the centre of Roman administration in Judea. The city was a Mediterranean port and commercial centre. A few Roman pillars, later used by the Crusaders in their own building work, can still be seen on the sea shore.

earlier trials of Jesus. In Jesus' case the original accusation of the Jews was a religious one, which was altered to a political one before the Roman judge, so that a definite charge could be brought under Roman law.

Though Felix, like every other Roman official, disliked anything that might cause disorder, he was convinced of Paul's innocence. He postponed his decision on the case, partly in the hope of receiving a bribe from Paul and partly for fear of arousing yet more trouble among the Jews if Paul was found innocent.

Acts 24:1–26

Festus hears Paul

At this point (about AD 59) Felix himself was recalled to Rome to give account of his behaviour in other affairs. The new procurator was a man called Porcius Festus, who heard Paul's case again. He suggested another trial in Jerusalem, something that was quite unthinkable to Paul. He knew the risk of assassination there, and he could also foresee further delays. His imprisonment had already lasted two years. Paul knew that he must reach his ultimate goal, Rome. If he had to go there as a prisoner, so it would have to be. So he decided to exercise his right of appeal to

Paul's voyage to Rome

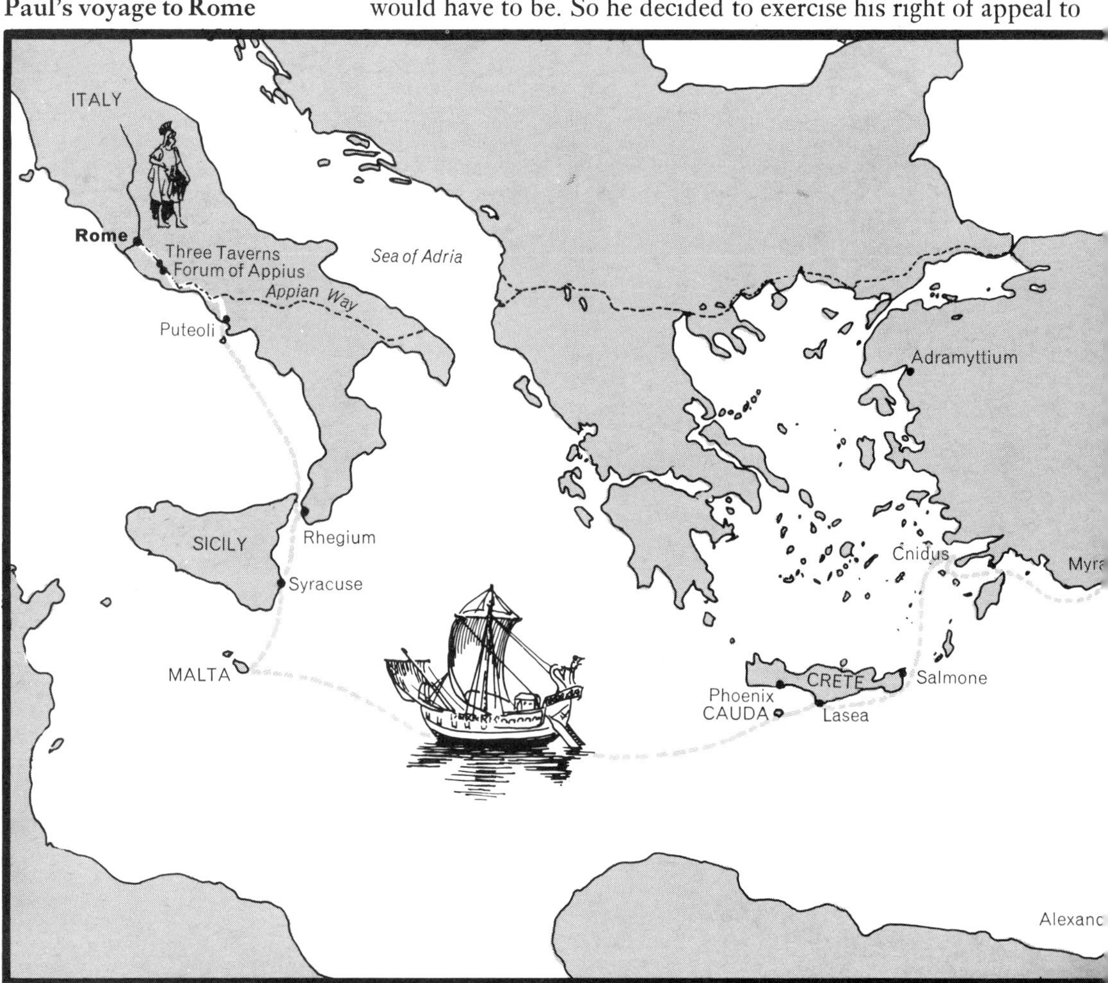

Acts 25:1–12

the supreme court of the Roman Empire: the emperor himself in Rome.

Festus was completely unsettled by Paul's appeal to Rome, for he realized the weakness of the case against Paul and was at a loss to know what to write to the emperor. When Herod Agrippa II visited Ceasarea, Paul was again called to appear before both men in the hope that Agrippa, who knew more about Jewish affairs, would be able to suggest a solution. Both rulers appear to have been very impressed with Paul's message, though they tried to pass it off by joking about it.

Acts 26:1–32

Destination Rome

At last Paul got his heart's desire, and he was sent off to Rome accompanied by Luke and another of his friends, Aristarchus. He travelled on a ship full of convicted criminals. Such 'prison ships' were making regular voyages from Palestine to Rome at this time. The Romans kept the amphitheatres in Rome operating by the import of wretched criminals from elsewhere in the empire. The criminals probably preferred a 'heroic' death with gladiators or wild animals in the arena to the slow and painful process of crucifixion.

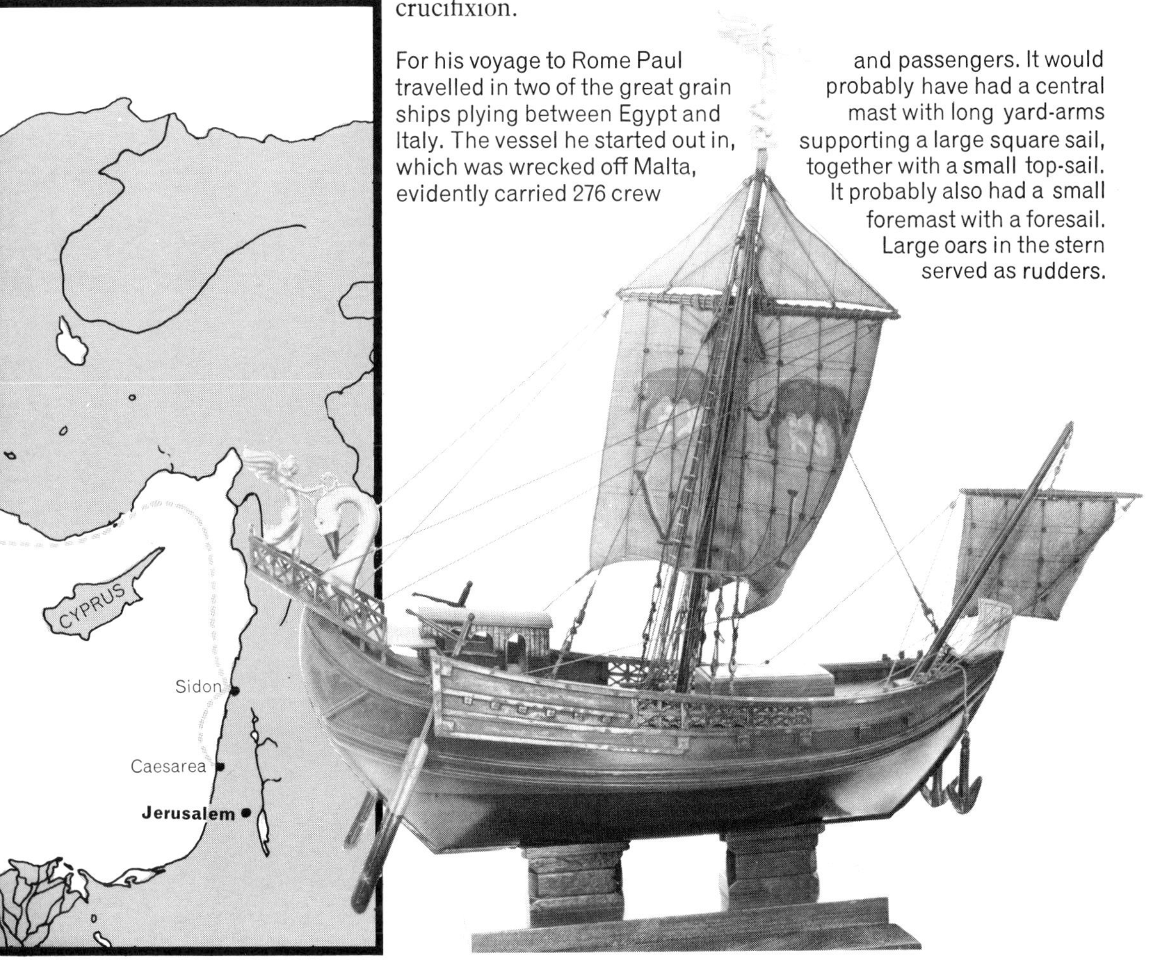

For his voyage to Rome Paul travelled in two of the great grain ships plying between Egypt and Italy. The vessel he started out in, which was wrecked off Malta, evidently carried 276 crew and passengers. It would probably have had a central mast with long yard-arms supporting a large square sail, together with a small top-sail. It probably also had a small foremast with a foresail. Large oars in the stern served as rudders.

Paul seems to have been treated as a special case. The fact that he had two companions with him suggests he was travelling in the style of a well-to-do Roman, accompanied by two of his slaves. The fact that he could be consulted about the details of the voyage also suggests that Paul had a special position. The voyage to Rome, with its storms and shipwrecks, is one of the most graphic descriptions of such an experience in all ancient literature, and is obviously a first-hand account of the journey.

Acts 27:9–12

Acts 27:1–28:13

After many adventures on the way, Paul eventually landed at Puteoli in southern Italy, where he was warmly welcomed by the local Christians. As he got nearer Rome some of the Christians even came out some distance along the road to meet him. For two years Paul remained a prisoner. But he was permitted to live in a house rented by himself along with some Roman guards, whom he would also have had to pay.

Acts 28:14

Acts 28:15

Even in such unusual circumstances, however, Paul still did not lose sight of the commission given to him by the risen Lord. He knew that it was not really the Jews or the Romans who had sent

St Paul's Bay, Malta, ties in with the description of the site of Paul's shipwreck in Acts 27:39–41. A shallow sandbank runs out and is probably where the ship struck and began breaking up. The crew and passengers used timber from the ship to float ashore on the calmer water inside the spit. Paul continued his journey to Rome in the Alexandrian ship Castor and Pollux.

Opposite. After Paul landed in Italy Christians came out from Rome to meet him at the Forum of Appius on the Appian Way. This famous Roman road is still lined with Roman monuments.

him to Rome: it was God. Paul had planned to come to the capital city and, although he could hardly have foreseen the nature of his arrival, he knew that Christ had specifically instructed him to 'bear witness also at Rome'.

Acts 23:11

Rome at last

Accordingly, Paul soon got in contact with the leaders of the Jewish community there. As in other places, when they heard his message some of them believed but the majority rejected it. So Paul again turned to the Gentiles. In spite of the limitations imposed by his house arrest, the last picture we see of him is of a

It is unclear how the Christian church in Rome came into existence. It included people from Greek, Roman and Jewish backgrounds, and some from the Emperor's household. The Forum, seen here, stood with the other major public buildings at the city centre. Rome at this time had a population of over one million.

man still living in complete obedience to the call he had been given so many years before. He was at last in the centre of the empire, 'preaching the kingdom of God and teaching about the Lord Jesus Christ quite openly and unhindered'.

Acts 28:31

Paul had achieved his objective. The risen Lord had sent him out as the apostle to the Gentiles. His job was 'to open their eyes, that they may turn from darkness to light and from the power of Satan to God, that they may receive forgiveness of sins and a place among those who are sanctified by faith in me'. As Paul reached Rome, he knew that he had fulfilled the terms of his commission. He approached the 'eternal city' with the satisfaction of knowing that in every strategic centre throughout the whole of the then-known world there was a group of people who had experienced the enlightenment brought by the Christian message; people whose lives were directed, as his had been, by the risen Christ.

Acts 26:18

When did Paul die?

The story in Acts ends at the point where Paul arrived in Rome. Luke was more interested in recounting the progress of the Christian message from Jerusalem to Rome than in the messengers whom God chose to spread the good news. But all the traditions of the early church say that Paul met a martyr's death at Rome during the persecution ordered by Nero in AD 64. We may suppose that, despite the long delays, he was ultimately brought to trial at Rome. Perhaps he was sentenced to death immediately after this, though in view of the reluctance of Felix and Festus even to send him for trial it is unlikely that he could have been found guilty on the charges under which he was sent to the emperor's court.

Since this trial would take place about AD 62, Paul presumably engaged in other activities until his final trial and death under Nero in AD 64. This is certainly the view taken by early church tradition. Eusebius, one of the early church historians, tells us that 'after defending himself the apostle was sent again on his ministry of preaching, and coming a second time to the same city, suffered martyrdom under Nero' (*Ecclesiastical History*, ii. 22). There are two possibilities for his further activities:

- One is that Paul fulfilled his intention of going on to Spain. There is no biblical evidence to support this. But there are traditions in Spain itself to this effect, and also a statement that he did so in 1 *Clement* 5 (a letter written about AD 95 by Clement of Rome to the church at Corinth). But it is more likely that the originators of these traditions based their statements on what Paul said in Romans 15:24, and assumed that since he wanted to visit Spain he must actually have done so.
- The other possibility concerning what Paul did after his supposed release arises from the references to Paul's travels in the Pastoral Epistles (1 and 2 Timothy and Titus). These letters may suggest that Paul again revisited some of the places he had been to earlier in Asia Minor and Greece, and also some others of which there is no mention in Acts or in the earlier letters, such as Colossae, Crete and Nicopolis.

It is not essential to assume that such visits took place towards the end of Paul's life, for Acts by no means gives us a complete account of all Paul's earlier travels. In 2 Corinthians 11:23–27 he speaks of many incidents not mentioned in Acts, but which had presumably occurred in the course of his pastoral ministry in Ephesus and the surrounding areas. Nevertheless, it would take a considerable amount of ingenuity to fit the travel references of the Pastoral Epistles into the Acts narrative. It is certainly easier to suppose that they represent further missionary exploits after his first visit to Rome. But even then it is by no means easy to fit all these references into a plausible journey. There are also other difficulties involved in understanding the Pastoral Epistles, which are dealt with in the next chapter.

7 Paul in Prison

IN FOUR of his letters (apart from 2 Timothy) Paul refers to himself as a prisoner. So it is generally assumed that they were written during his period of imprisonment at Rome from AD 60–62. These are the letters to the churches at Colossae, Philippi and Ephesus, and the personal letter to Philemon, who lived at Colossae.

Paul writes to the church at Colossae

Colossians and Philemon were written at the same time as each other, the former to the church and the latter to one member of it. Timothy is associated with Paul as the author of them both, and there are greetings in both from the same five people. Aristarchus, Mark, Demas, Epaphras, Luke and Archippus of Colossae are mentioned in both, and so is Philemon's runaway slave, Onesimus.

Though Colossae was not too far from Ephesus, where Paul had worked for three years, he had never visited the town. The church at Colossae had probably been founded by Epaphras, who may have been one of Paul's converts in Ephesus. The fact that such a thriving church had been established at Colossae by this time is striking proof of the wisdom of Paul's missionary strategy of establishing his own work in a central place from which other Christians could reach out to the surrounding areas.

Epaphras visited Paul during his imprisonment in Rome, and gave him a generally encouraging report of the Colossian church. But one thing was causing him real concern. This was the spread

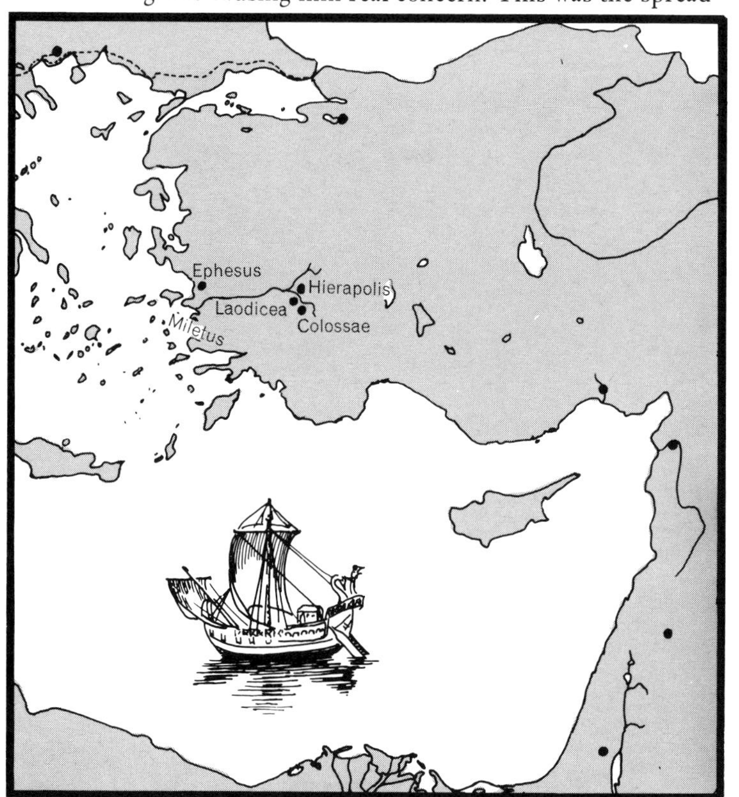

Towns of the Lycus Valley

Several of Paul's later letters were written to Christians in this area (Colossians, Ephesians and Philemon)

of a false teaching which today we often call 'the Colossian heresy'. It was a combination of the practices Paul was opposing when he wrote Galatians with the sort of beliefs held by the 'Christ party' in Corinth. The racial exclusivism of people like the Judaizers had been combined with the intellectual exclusivism common in many pagan religious cults of the day. As a result a group of people in the Colossian church considered themselves better Christians then the rest of the church members. These people held that a complete and lasting salvation could not be achieved simply by faith in Christ, as Paul had taught. In addition to having faith in Christ, it was also necessary to obtain an

Colossae stood in the broad fertile valley of the Lycus, near Laodicea. The ancient town is now buried beneath a mound – in the background in this picture of modern Turkey.

insight into divine things through a secret knowledge given in a mystical way.

Such knowledge could be acquired by taking part in various ritual practices, such as circumcision, not eating certain foods, and observing Jewish festivals and sabbaths. We can see that in practice the Colossian heretics must have seemed very similar to the Judaizers who led astray Paul's converts in Galatia. For they were also wanting to impose circumcision and other Jewish rituals. But the keeping of Old Testament principles among these Colossian Christians was in fact quite different from the teaching of the Judaizers. The Galatians had been tempted to observe the Old Testament Law as an integral part of keeping the religious covenants of the Old Testament. The Judaizers had told them they could not be a part of God's people unless they first became Jews, by accepting the claims of the Old Testament Law.

Colossians 2:23

But here in Colossae the heretics were keeping such rules for quite different reasons. They were 'ascetics'; what they wanted was something that would help them to check 'the indulgence of the flesh'. They were not 'legalists' like the Judaizers; the fact that they chose to achieve their asceticism by using certain parts of the Old Testament Law was only coincidence. This is very clear from Paul's reply to them. He deals not with the issues of law and grace (as in Galatians), but with the basic moral issues raised by any kind of ascetic practice.

Colossians

In his letter to the Colossian church, Paul deals with this false teaching by emphasizing again that in Christ the believer could find all he needed. Like the later Gnostics, some of the Colossians had been suggesting that they needed other supernatural agencies, and that Jesus was just one of several possible manifestations of God. Against this, Paul firmly asserts that 'In Christ all the fulness of God was pleased to dwell' (Colossians 1:19). Indeed, he went further than this by reminding his readers that in Jesus 'the whole fulness of deity dwells *bodily*' (2:9).

The Colossians claimed they needed to experience something deep and mysterious if they were to find full salvation, and Paul agreed with them. His own job could be described as the presentation of 'the mystery'. But far from being something deep and hidden, this 'mystery' was the very thing that lay at the heart of all Paul's preaching: the simple fact of Christ's own life within them (1:27). Whatever the Christian may need, it can all be found in Christ, for in him 'are hid all the treasures of wisdom and knowledge' (2:3).

Paul then went on to remind his readers of all the things they had as Christians, some of which they were now trying to achieve by other, mystical means.

● Were some of them claiming to be super-spiritual because they were circumcised? All Christians, says Paul, have received 'a circumcision made without hands' (2:11) when they fulfilled the true meaning of the old ceremony by 'putting off the body of flesh', that is their old sinful lives, that they might live a new life in the power of the Holy Spirit given to them by Christ.

● Was someone claiming to have a new kind of life that other Christians did not have? Then he should recognize that all Christians have been made alive by God through what Christ did on the cross (2:13–15).

● What about ritual observances, designed to keep 'the flesh' in subjection? These also are of no real value. Even in terms of their own original purpose they have been superseded. They were but 'a shadow of what is to come'. Since the reality has now come in Christ, they are no longer valid. In practice they were a waste of time. For though they may have 'an appearance of wisdom in promoting rigour of devotion and self-abasement and severity to the body . . . they are of no value in checking the indulgence of the flesh' (2:23).

Instead of fixing their attention on these things, the Colossians ought to live up to their true position in Christ. Whoever they are, and whatever experiences they claim to have, all Christians stand equal before God. All have the same temptations to face (3:5–11), and there is only one way for all of them to overcome such temptations: 'Set your minds on things that are above, not on things that are on earth. For you have died, and your life is hid with Christ in God . . . Hence there cannot be Greek and Jew, circumcised and uncircumcised, barbarian, Scythian, slave, free man, but Christ is all, and in all' (3:2–3, 11).

Instead of following a false set of values based on their own worthless speculations, the Colossians ought again to remind themselves that the true ambition of the Christian must be to become like Christ (3:12–17): 'Whatever you do, in word or deed, do everything in the name of the Lord Jesus, giving thanks to God the Father through him' (3:17).

By their emphasis on asceticism and speculation the Colossian heretics had taken the Christian faith out of real life. But Paul was convinced, as always, that the Christian faith must be a faith for realistic living. So he ends his letter by showing how the power of Christ that lives in the Christian (1:27) works itself out in the family (3:18–21), at work (3:22–4:1), in the church (4:2–4), and in life in general (4:5–6).

Paul writes to the Ephesian churches

Colossians 4:16

There is in Colossians a reference to another letter: 'When this letter has been read among you, have it read also in the church of the Laodiceans; and see that you read also the letter from Laodicea'. Laodicea was another town quite near to Colossae, and Paul wanted the churches to exchange letters.

There is, of course, no 'letter to the Laodiceans' contained in our New Testament. Noting this omission, the church of the early centuries lost no time in producing such a letter. We know a Latin version; it may also have been available in Greek. There is every reason to suppose that this letter (which is almost impossible to date accurately) is a forgery. It contains no theology, and consists of a series of bits and pieces from Paul's other letters strung together in an aimless way.

Most modern scholars believe we do in fact possess a copy of 'the letter from Laodicea' to which Paul referred – namely the letter in our New Testament known as Ephesians. This letter contains in a fuller and more carefully argued form the same kind of teaching about the person of Christ as in Colossians, but without the pointed references to the local Colossian heresy.

Three other things also suggest that this letter to the Ephesians was probably intended for other churches in the area as well as for the Christians at Ephesus:

● The words 'at Ephesus' in Ephesians 1:1 (the only indication that the letter was destined for that city) are not found in our best and oldest manuscripts of this letter. The Revised Standard Version of the New Testament puts the words 'at Ephesus' in the margin.

● There are no personal greetings in this letter, though Paul probably had more friends in Ephesus than anywhere else.

● The second-century heretic Marcion called our Ephesians 'the letter to the Laodiceans'.

We may therefore suggest that Ephesians was a circular letter addressed to a number of different congregations. The words 'at Ephesus' in Ephesians 1:1 would be found in the copy that went to that city, while the copy referred to in Colossians 4:16 would have the words 'at Laodicea' instead.

Ephesians

In Ephesians, Paul again emphasizes the central place of Christ in the plan of God and in the life of the Christian believer. He begins by reminding his readers of the great privileges they possess in Christ. Though the people to whom he was writing had previously 'lived in the passions of' their flesh (Ephesians 2:3), God had put them in a new position. They had been 'made . . . alive together with Christ . . . and raised . . . up with him, and made to sit with him in the heavenly places' (2:5–6). Every individual Christian had become a part of God's new creation in which he planned 'to unite all things in Christ, things in heaven and things on earth' (1:10).

Some of the people who read Paul's letter had been told these things before by Paul himself. For this was his special ministry: 'to preach to the Gentiles the unsearchable riches of Christ' (3:8); and to demonstrate how those 'riches' could be received and enjoyed in real life. Some of his readers may have been influenced by false teaching like the Colossian heresy. They would find the true satisfaction they desired only if they were willing to be 'filled with all the fullness of God' (3:19), which is found nowhere else but in Christ.

After setting out this profound description of Christ as Saviour of the world and as the source of all physical, mental and spiritual knowledge and activity, Paul went on to draw out the practical implications of all this. If his readers were indeed members of Christ's body, new men and children of God, they must show by their actions who they really are:

● In the church they should be 'eager to maintain the unity of the Spirit in the bond of peace' (4:3). As in 1 Corinthians 12, Paul again says that they could expect the unity of the Spirit to be displayed by the giving of 'gifts' to 'the body' for its growth and development (4:7–16). Because Christians are united with one another in the church fellowship, any wrong done by one member will inevitably affect the others. This would 'grieve the Holy Spirit of God' (4:30). In view of what God had done for them in Christ, Christians ought to 'be kind to one another, tenderhearted, forgiving one another, as God in Christ forgave' them (4:32). Paul could even advise them to 'be imitators of God' (5:1), by showing in their dealings with one another the same self-sacrificing love as God had shown to them in Christ.

● In personal morality Christians should 'take no part in the unfruitful works of darkness' (5:11). What ought to characterize them is that they are 'filled with the Spirit' (5:18), the results of which Paul had listed in Galatians 5:22–23.

In Paul's time most books came in the form of a scroll – a long roll of parchment or papyrus. The reader would unroll one end and roll up the other as he read.

● In their social life Christians must again be ruled by the principle of self-giving love, whether the matter at issue is in the family (5:21–6:4) or at work (6:5–9).

Finally, Paul reminded his readers that in their life as Christians they would encounter opposition, 'the wiles of the devil', against which they must 'put on the whole armour of God' (6:11).

As an ethical theory, what Paul had put forward here would be impossible to carry out. How could a man or woman be ruled by self-sacrificing love of the same kind that God had shown in Christ? Paul knew from his own personal experience and his knowledge of the experience of others, that it was possible in only one way: if the Christian was 'strong in the Lord and in the strength of his might' (6:10). This was a lesson that Paul had emphasized in the first letter he wrote, and a lifetime of work for Christ had only strengthened his belief that 'if we live by the Spirit', we ought also to 'walk by the Spirit' (Galatians 5:25).

Paul writes to the church at Philippi

Paul brought out the same lesson in the other letter he wrote from prison: Philippians. With the exception of Philemon, this is the most personal of Paul's letters. It was written to acknowledge a gift that the Philippian church had sent to Paul to help him financially while in Rome. One of the Philippian Christians, a man called Epaphroditus, had brought the gift from Philippi and had been a great help to Paul during his short stay in Rome. Most of Paul's letter, which was sent back to Philippi with Epaphroditus, is concerned with personal matters affecting Paul's possible release, and expressing his warm affection for the Philippian Christians.

● Differences within the church. There was just one problem in the church at Philippi that Paul felt he should deal with in his letter. One or two minor disagreements had arisen, especially between two women in the church, Euodia and Syntyche, but also probably in a more general way. Paul's advice to these people is found in what is one of the best-known parts of all his writings: the so-called 'Christ hymn'. It is generally thought that in referring to the humbling of Christ and his subsequent rise to glory, Paul was quoting from an early Christian hymn that would be familiar to his readers, and probably to Christians in other churches as well. This section certainly tends to interrupt the flow of Paul's language here. It also has the style of a hymn, with a definite rhythm, carefully balanced lines, and the 'parallelism' that was characteristic of Hebrew poetry.

Philippians 4:2–3

See Philippians 2:1–4

Philippians 2:5–11

● The example of Christ. But the 'Christ hymn' is also remarkable for another reason. It is the only place in Paul's letters (except for 2 Corinthians 8:9–10, which is almost identical to this) where Paul gives the example of Jesus as a pattern for Christian behaviour.

Modern preachers who tell their listeners to follow Christ's example usually have in mind the kind of things that Jesus did during his ministry. The Gospels provide countless examples of Christ's compassion, care and good works. But it is quite striking that Paul never urged Christians to follow this example. In those places where he did give Christ as an example for Christians to follow, the example he chose was Christ's giving up all that was his when he became man. This idea was very important for Paul, and lay at the heart of his theology. In order to be a Christian at all a person must be prepared to give up himself and all that he is completely to Christ. This was the lesson he had learnt on the Damascus road, when he responded in faith to the demands of the risen Christ. It runs like a golden thread through all his letters.

When was Paul imprisoned?

In our consideration of Paul's life and letters, we have assumed that those letters which indicate Paul was a prisoner when he wrote them were written from Rome between AD 60 and AD 62. This is the only imprisonment recorded in Acts, and it has been natural for readers of Paul's letters from the earliest times to assume that they were written at this time.

Following the lead given by Professor G. S. Duncan, some scholars now think that at least one or two of these four letters were written not from Rome but during an unrecorded imprisonment at Ephesus, which took place during Paul's three-year stay there. There is a considerable amount of evidence that makes such an imprisonment likely.

2 Corinthians 11:23, written towards the end of Paul's stay in Ephesus, informs us that by comparison with other Christian workers he had experienced 'far greater labours, far more imprisonments, with countiess beatings, and often near death'. In 1 Corinthians 15:32 Paul wrote that he 'fought with beasts at Ephesus', a phrase which we saw to be a figure of speech and could probably describe a trial preceding imprisonment. Again, 2 Corinthians 1:8 speaks of 'the affliction we experienced in Asia', the Roman province of which Ephesus was the capital. In addition Romans 16:7, written shortly after he left Ephesus, refers to two people as 'my fellow prisoners'.

Other evidence that Paul was imprisoned at Ephesus is to be found in the Latin introductions to New Testament books that were written in the second century under the influence of the Gnostic Marcion. Also the fictitious second-century *Acts of Paul* tells of an imprisonment of Paul at Ephesus, followed by an encounter with lions in the arena, from which he was delivered by supernatural intervention.

Arguments for an imprisonment at Ephesus

The combination of this kind of evidence with the clues in Paul's own writings makes it fairly probable that he did suffer a period of imprisonment during his three-year stay in Ephesus. The fact that Paul may have been imprisoned there does not, of course, make it necessary to believe that he wrote the 'prison letters' from Ephesus. But more positive arguments have been put forward to support this view:

- It is claimed that the friends of Paul who are mentioned as having made contact with him during this imprisonment would be more likely to have been in Ephesus than in Rome, which was a long way from their homes. Against this must be set the fact that we know next to nothing about most of these associates of Paul. The one of whom we know most, Luke, was certainly with Paul in Rome though, according to Acts, not in Ephesus.
- It is argued that Philemon's slave Onesimus would be more likely to run away to Ephesus, which was only about eighty miles from his home in Colossae than to Rome, which would be almost 800 miles away. This again is not a convincing argument; for at that time all roads literally did lead to Rome. A runaway slave would be more likely to try to disappear in the capital of the empire than in a provincial town the size of Ephesus.
- In Philippians we get the impression that there was much travelling to and from Paul's prison; and Ephesus was much nearer to Philippi than Rome. This is often taken to be a strong argument for supposing that Philippians at least must have been written from Ephesus.
- The strongest argument for an Ephesian origin of these letters is that in them Paul was looking forward to an early release, after which he intended visiting his friends in both Philippi and Colossae. In Romans 15:28, however, he had made it plain that after his visit to Jerusalem his intention was not to revisit churches he had founded before, but to go west to Spain.

What then can we conclude from these facts? It is almost certain that Paul did have a period of imprisonment during his stay in Ephesus. It is quite possible that Philippians at least, with its mention of frequent journeys between Philippi and Paul's prison, may have been written at this time. If this was the case, we would need to date the letter to the Philippians about AD 55 instead of AD 62.

Paul and the risen Christ

Galatians 2:20

Galatians 1:21

Galatians 3:8

In his first letter, the key to much of Paul's argument was found in his conviction that 'I have been crucified with Christ; it is no longer I who live, but Christ who lives in me . . .'. As he lived under house arrest in Rome, writing to the Philippian church, Paul again set the dominant note by his simple yet profound statement, just five words in Greek, 'For to me to live is Christ.' Between these two statements lay a lifetime of Christian experience. Paul had seen what the risen Christ could do with a man's life and talents if they were submitted to the supreme lordship of Christ.

No wonder then that Paul laid such an emphasis on the power that was available to him through the work of the risen Christ in his own life. It had revolutionized the whole course of his career. He knew that it would do the same for all his converts if they were willing to say with him, 'I count everything as loss because of the surpassing worth of knowing Christ Jesus my Lord.'

It was something of this sort that Paul was saying in all the letters he wrote from prison.

Did Paul write the Pastoral Epistles?

The three letters which we refer to under the combined title 'the Pastoral Epistles' (1 and 2 Timothy and Titus) are very different from Paul's other letters. They were written not to churches, but to two individuals who were working among groups of young Christians: Timothy at Ephesus and Titus in Crete. In form, subject-matter and style these three letters are very similar to each other. But in all these respects they are quite distinct from Paul's other letters. The differences are so striking that many scholars today say that these three letters could not have been written by Paul himself.

In considering this question, four main points need to be taken into consideration:

Paul's movements

It is difficult to fit the movements of Paul shown in these letters into the story of his doings in Acts. Three main reasons have therefore been given to explain the historical references made in these letters:

● First, that *Paul was released after the imprisonment recorded in Acts.* He continued his missionary work for a period of about two years before meeting his death in Rome. No such release is recorded in Acts. But that is no real stumbling-block since Luke's purpose was not to write a biography of Paul but to tell how the Christian message had spread from small beginnings in Jerusalem to the centre of the empire in Rome. The view that Paul was released and carried on further work has been the traditional view since the earliest days of the church, and is still held today by some scholars. But even working on this assumption, it is still very difficult to string together all the travel references made in the Pastoral Epistles to produce any sensible sort of 'journey'.

● Secondly, noting this, radical nineteenth-century scholars such as F. C. Baur made the suggestion that *these letters were second-century writings* by people who were trying to reinterpret Paul at a time when he had fallen out of favour with the church. These people simply invented the travel references of the Pastorals to give a touch of realism to their own work. The difficulty with this view is that the historical references contained in these letters are not the kind of thing that anyone would invent. Take, for instance, 2 Timothy 4:13, 'When you come, bring the cloak that I left with Carpus at Troas, also the books, and above all the parchments.' This is not the kind of detail that a later 'Paulinist' would invent. It has no theological content and tells us nothing essential about Paul himself. It is far more likely that it originated in some real-life situation.

● Thirdly, other scholars, recognizing this difficulty, have suggested that, though the letters in their present form were written in the second century by someone who was trying to re-assert the authority of Paul in the church, they do *contain genuine Pauline fragments*, such as the piece to which we have referred. Dr P. N. Harrison suggested that five genuine scraps of Paul's writings can be discovered in 2 Timothy and Titus, and that these were fitted into his own work by a second-century writer. A majority of modern scholars accept this view.

But it is difficult to see how or why five such fragments should have had an independent existence from the time of Paul in the middle of the first century to the time of his imitator almost a hundred years later. Since they contain nothing more than scraps of personal information, it is hard to think that anyone would have been interested in preserving them intact, had they been isolated from other more theological teaching.

Paul probably dictated his letters to a secretary, sometimes adding a personal greeting at the end. This wooden pen-case contains reed-pens and an inkwell half-full of black ink, and dates from Paul's time.

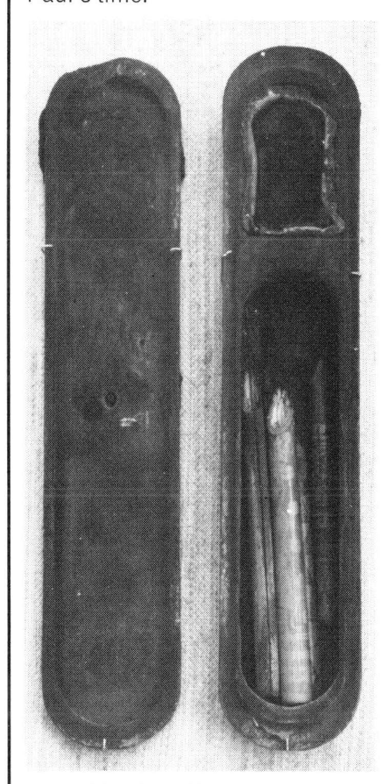

Church organization

Attention is often drawn to the fact that the type of church organization shown in these letters is much more developed than the organization seen in Paul's earlier letters. Therefore the Pastoral Epistles reflect something like the second-century church with its ruling bishops and complicated organization. This argument can easily be disposed of:

● In Paul's earlier letters he was not writing directly about the duties of church officers. So we need not be surprised to find that letters which deal with this subject give the appearance of a more organized kind of church.

● No church officers are mentioned in the Pastoral Epistles that are not mentioned either in Acts or in Paul's earlier letters.

● The position of Timothy and Titus is not that of the 'monarchical' or ruling bishop. Rather are they Paul's personal messengers. Their authority stems from the fact that he was an apostle, and they had been sent as his representatives.

● This whole argument has usually been based on the suggestion that some sort of Gnostic heresy was in view in the Pastoral Epistles and so they must be second-century works. But it is now widely recognized by all scholars that the kind of Gnosticism found in the second century *cannot* be found in these letters. What Timothy and Titus were opposing was not too different from the kind of thing that Paul faced earlier in Corinth and Colossae.

Doctrinal teaching

Some scholars say that the Pastoral Epistles contain very little of Paul's characteristic doctrinal teaching, except for a few statements called 'faithful sayings' (for example 1 Timothy 1:15). The doctrine of the Holy Spirit is not mentioned here, and whereas in Paul's day the life of the church was directed by the Spirit, or 'charismatic', in the Pastorals it seems to be organizational. Therefore it must reflect a later stage of church development. Two things can be said here:

● We must beware of thinking that Paul's 'charismatic' doctrine led to a free-for-all in the church. Far from it. When Paul spoke of the spiritual gifts (*charismata*) in 1 Corinthians 12–14 he clearly meant to imply that there should be order and position within the church. Not every man and woman would be equipped by the Spirit to perform the same work. Philippians 1:1 and 1 Thessalonians 5:12 show that Paul approved of formal leadership in the church, and according to Acts 14:23 he himself appointed elders. Such men and women ought to be Spirit-directed and empowered. But that did not mean there was no formal or visible order about the way in which they operated.

● It is not true to say that the Holy Spirit has no part to play in the Pastoral Epistles. We find here the same emphasis on the working of the Holy Spirit in the life of believers (2 Timothy 1:14). Timothy himself is said to have been appointed as God's servant by means of prophecy, which was one of the most characteristic ways of the Spirit's working (1 Timothy 1:18).

Style and vocabulary

The real strength of the suggestion that the Pastoral Epistles were not written by Paul lies in the style and vocabulary of the letters. There are about 175 words here which are not found in Paul's other letters. Dr Harrison has argued that all of these are more characteristic of second-century Christian writers than of first-century writers. In addition to these words, there is a difference of style in what might be called the 'connecting tissue' of these letters, that is the arrangement of 'ands' and 'buts' and other conjunctions. This is rather different from Paul's other letters, and 112 of his favourite particles and prepositions are missing.

These facts are impressive, and should not be set aside lightly. Nevertheless, we may doubt whether they decide the question. Some linguistic experts think that the Pastoral Epistles are too short to provide us with enough material to carry out a trustworthy literary analysis of this kind. And even if the method is valid, both style and vocabulary are very often affected by the subject-matter that is being discussed. Even the argument from the use of typical connecting particles is not wholly convincing, for Colossians and 2 Thessalonians both have considerably fewer of these than Paul's other letters.

What Dr Harrison has shown is that there are differences between the language of the Pastorals and Paul's earlier letters. These differences could perhaps be explained by reference to the different subject-matter, to the fact that Paul was now an older man, or even to the fact that he was using a different secretary. It is also possible that the style of a letter written by Paul himself may have been revised later to make it into better Greek.

The argument for and against Paul's authorship of these letters is very finely balanced, and there is perhaps as much to be said on the one side as on the other. All the evidence of the early church writings supports the view that Paul was the author of these letters. Whatever view we choose regarding their present form, we must admit that their content is such as Paul could have written. If he was the author in the same sense as he was the author of the earlier letters, he must have written to Timothy and Titus some time between AD 62 and AD 64.

8 'A Man in Christ'

IN THE first chapter of this book, we tried to answer the question 'Who was Paul?' We can now ask the same question again in the light of what we have learnt from his life and letters.

Who was Paul?

To the Judaizers of the Galatian churches, Paul was a Pharisee who had thrown aside the Jewish Law. He had perverted its inner meaning by suggesting that it had been superseded by the coming of Jesus, whom Paul believed to be the promised Messiah of the Old Testament. For them, Paul was the man who was contradicting the very basis of Old Testament religion. He was suggesting that Christians could live without law of any sort – something that the Judaizers thought would lead inevitably to moral anarchy in the Gentile churches.

To many of the Gentile Christians, on the other hand, Paul still seemed to be very much a Jew. Perhaps a liberated Jew, but one who could not escape the inborn prejudices which characterized his race. Though he claimed he had been released from having to obey the letter of the Law, they felt his actions often did not match up to his beliefs. Otherwise, why should he have got so upset about some of the Corinthian Christians entering fully into the moral and spiritual freedom which they believed his message had given them?

In Paul's own view, his position lay somewhere between these two extremes. It is quite certain that he never forgot his birth from the royal tribe of Benjamin, nor his good education as a Pharisee. In spite of his own special call to be the apostle to the Gentiles, and his firm belief that in Christ there was neither Jew nor Gentile, Paul was still proud of being a Jew.

Paul's conversion

This pride gives us an added insight into the story of Paul's conversion. As a good Jew he rightly saw that the central idea of Judaism was obedience to the Law. If he was to reach both his true dignity as a Jew and his own ultimate salvation, he must go the whole way in obeying the Jewish Law (Torah). In Romans 7 we have an account, notable for its frankness and honesty, of the struggle that went on in Paul's own life. As he tried to keep the Law he found it to be an impossibility – a fact that drove him to despair from which the Law was helpless to save him. It was characteristic of Paul that when he found he could not fulfil the Law by obedience, he found another way of expressing his eager pride in Judaism; by persecuting the Christians, who to him were the arch-enemies of the Law.

But at his conversion Paul saw the risen Christ. He realized that the Law and all the other things on which he had previously relied were worthless compared to his new Lord and Master. The discovery that his own salvation depended neither on his privileges as a Jew nor on his own ability to make himself morally acceptable to God revolutionized his whole outlook. His mission now became the proclamation of salvation through what Christ had already done—a message that was to be shared with the Gentiles, people whom as a Jew he had utterly despised, but who now became his brothers and sisters in Christ. Yet despite the unbelief of the Jews Paul was still convinced that they had a place in God's plan.

Romans 9–11

The epistle of the Apostle Saynct Paul to the Romayns.

The fyrst Chapter.

Paul the servaunt of Jesus Christ called to be an Apostle/put a parte to preache the Gospell of God/ which he promysed afore by his Prophetes/in the holy scriptures that make mension of his sonne/ the which was begotten of the seed of David/ as pertayninge to the fleshe:and declared to be the sonne of God / with power of the Holy goost that sanctifieth /sence the tyme that Jesus Christ oure Lorde rose agayne from deeth/ by whom we haue receaued grace and Apostleshyppe/to bringe all maner hethen people vnto the obedience of the fayth/ that is in his name: of the which hethen are ye a part also / which are Jesus Christes by vocacion.

To all you of Rome beloued of God & sayntes by callinge. Grace be with you & peace from God oure father/& from the lorde Jesus Christ.

Fyrst

To the Romayns Fo.clxxxvii

Fyrst verely I thanke my God thorow Jesus Christ/for you all/because youre fayth is published through out all the worlde. For God is my witnes/whom I serue with my sprete in the Gospell of his sonne/that with out ceasynge I make mencion of you allwayes in my prayers/ beseechynge that at one tyme or other a prosperous iorney (by the will of God) myght fortune me/to come vnto you. For I longe to see you/ that I myght bestowe amonge you some spirituall gyfte/to strenght you with all:that is/ that I myght haue consolacion to gether with you/ thorough the comen fayth/which both ye & I haue.

I wolde that ye shuld knowe brethren/how that I haue often tymes purposed to come vnto you (but haue bene let hytherto) to haue some frute amonge you/as I haue amonge other of the Gentyls. For I am detter both to the Grekes and to them which are no Grekes/vnto the learned and also vnto the vnlearned. Lykewyse/as moche as in me is/I am redy to preache the Gospell to you of Rome also.

For I am not ashamed of the gospell of Christ because it is the power of God vnto saluacion to all that beleue/namely to the Jewe/& also to the Gentyle. For by it the ryghtewesnes which cometh of God/is opened/from fayth to *fayth As it is written: The iust shall lyue by fayth.

For the wrath of God apereth from heauen agaynst all vngodlynes & vnryghtewesnes of men which withholde the trueth in vnryghtewesnes:seynge/ what maye be knowe of God/ that same is manifest amonge them. For God dyd shewe it vnto them. So that his invisible thinges:that is to saye his eternall power and godhed/are vnderstonde and sene/by the workes from the creacion of the worlde. So that they are without excuse/ in as moche as when they knewe God / they glorified him not as God/

a.iij. nether

Aba.ii.a Hebr.x. Gala.iii.

*From fayth to fayth/is as from a weake faith to a stronger/or from one batayle of fayth to another/for as we haue escaped one ieopardye thorow fayth/another invadeth us/thorow which we must wade by the helpe of fayth also.

Ephe.iiii.

Paul today

Modern thinkers have often taken a different attitude to Paul. The religious division between Jews and Gentiles is no longer so familiar to us today, nor is it important for us. It is therefore natural that scholars should have looked at Paul's life and teaching from a more detached viewpoint.

At one time it was fashionable to regard Paul as a theorizing theologian – the man responsible for changing the simple and practical religion of Jesus into a mass of obscure theology. This idea is quite false. Jesus was not just a simple ethical teacher. Paul's theology was not a philosophical system: it was what he worked out in the course of his own Christian experience. If he had not come up against the Judaizers in the Galatian churches, we should not have had the letter to the Galatians with its explanation of the relationship of the Christian to the Old Testament Law. If there had been no 'parties' in Corinth, we would not have the equally important teaching of 1 and 2 Corinthians. And if Paul had not been involved in these arguments perhaps he would never have written Romans in precisely the way he did. Paul's theology was not something analyzed in the study; it was a way of life to be experienced in the world of everyday reality.

Above. Paul's letters have influenced the faith and thought of Christians throughout the last two thousand years. This is the opening chapter of Romans in William Tyndale's English Bible.

'A man in Christ'

2 Corinthians 12:2

What, then, was the heart of his theology? The supreme fact for Paul was that he was 'a man in Christ'. It was by being 'in Christ' that a person could be justified before God, and share the new life Jesus had come to bring. It was by being 'in Christ' that a person could die to sin and be raised to a new life, reconciled to God.

For Paul, the fact that he was 'a man in Christ' was not just a theological theory. It was something that he had himself experienced. From the moment when he met the risen Christ on the Damascus road, Paul knew that his life was to be ruled, guided and directed by this new Lord whom he had previously despised. What Paul received from this Lord was not a system of ethics or doctrine, but rather a new life. It was a life that gave victory over sin and created a new fellowship in which all social and spiritual barriers were removed and overcome.

It is here that Paul has most to teach us today. By allowing the living Christ to direct his life as Lord and Saviour, Paul found a personal satisfaction and peace that he could not find in legalistic religion. He found that in Christ he became truly human. He came to terms with the depths of his own being and for the first time began to realize the true meaning of life.

Part of that meaning was that God had created man for fellowship with himself. The realization of this fact led Paul to see that in Christ all the barriers that separate men and women could be removed – whether barriers of sex, race, or cultural and social background. The individual Christian's relationship to Christ was not just inward and spiritual. It was a relationship that naturally produced a new freedom of fellowship of a real and practical kind between all those who were 'in Christ Jesus'.

Galatians 3:28

Paul discovered that in Christ all barriers of sex, race, culture and class can be broken down.

Freedom from guilt

As a result of what Christ had done in dying on the cross and rising again, Paul was delivered from that most universal of all human problems, guilt. As he thought carefully about the kind of person he was, he realized, as most of us do, that he was not the kind of person he claimed to be. He also knew from experience that constant self-examination could never be the answer to his guilty feelings. But through what Christ had done for him he had found deliverance from guilt, and a new aim in life that made living intensely worthwhile.

It was once fashionable to suppose that the guilt that Paul speaks about was simply the result of his Jewish upbringing – and that was often taken as a good reason for paying little attention to his Christian beliefs. But psychologists today agree that this is far from true, and that guilt is nothing less than the common heritage of the entire human race.

The psychologists put forward various explanations for this, and they are far from agreed as to the reasons for it. Paul had no doubt that *his* explanation of the origin of his guilt was the right

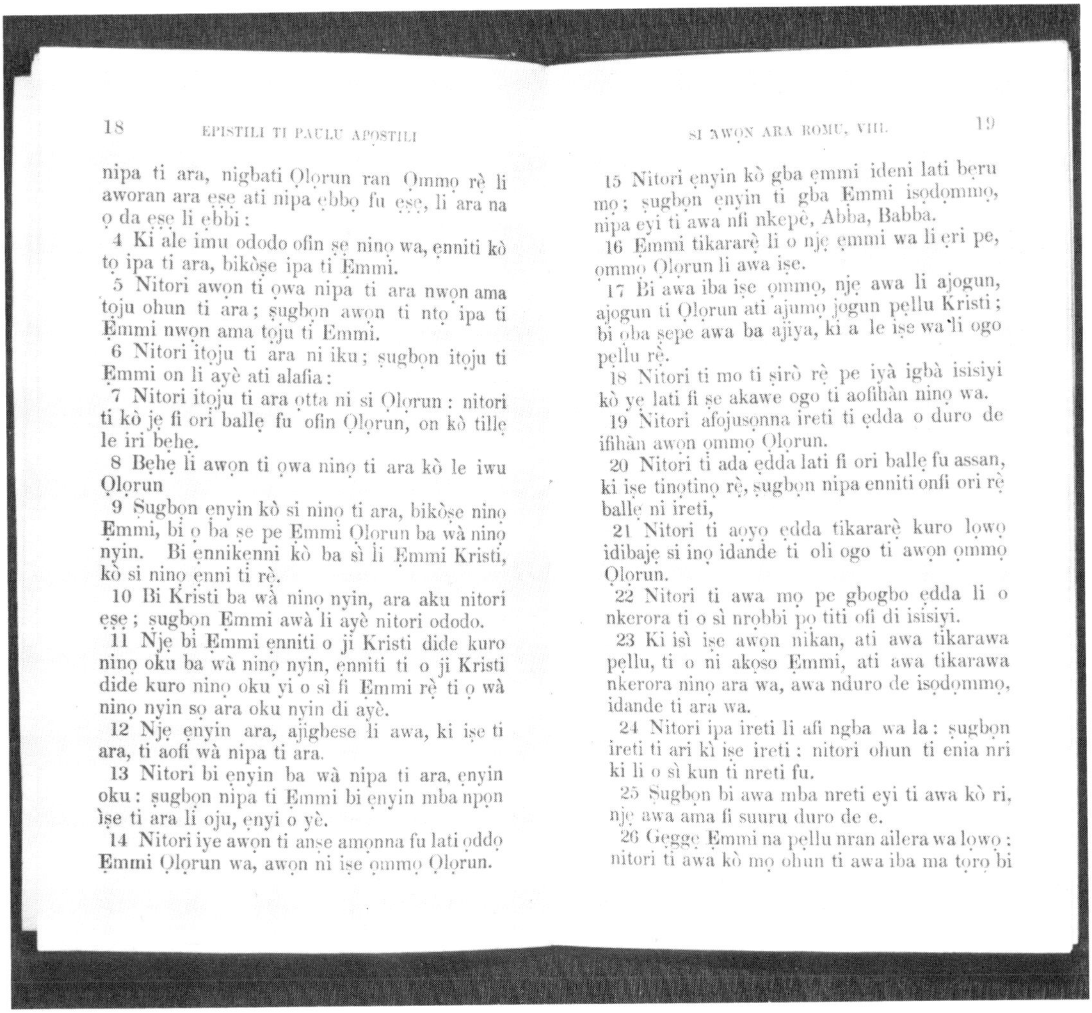

18 EPISTILI TI PAULU APOSTILI

nipa ti ara, nigbati Ọlọrun ran Ọmmọ rẹ̀ li aworan ara ẹṣẹ ati nipa ẹbbọ fu ẹṣẹ, li ara na ọ da ẹṣẹ li ẹbbi:

4 Ki ale imu ododo ofin ṣẹ ninọ wa, ẹnniti kò tọ ipa ti ara, bikòṣe ipa ti Ẹmmi.

5 Nitori awọn ti ọwa nipa ti ara nwọn ama tọju ohun ti ara; ṣugbọn awọn ti ntọ ipa ti Ẹmmi nwọn ama tọju ti Ẹmmi.

6 Nitori itọju ti ara ni iku; ṣugbọn itọju ti Ẹmmi on li ayè ati alafia:

7 Nitori itọju ti ara ọtta ni si Ọlọrun: nitori ti kò jẹ fi ori ballẹ fu ofin Ọlọrun, on kò tillẹ le iri bẹhẹ.

8 Bẹhẹ li awọn ti ọwa ninọ ti ara kò le iwu Ọlọrun

9 Ṣugbọn ẹnyin kò si ninọ ti ara, bikòṣe ninọ Ẹmmi, bi ọ ba ṣe pe Ẹmmi Ọlọrun ba wà ninọ nyin. Bi ẹnnikẹnni kò ba sì li Ẹmmi Kristi, kò si ninọ ẹnni ti rẹ̀.

10 Bi Kristi ba wà ninọ nyin, ara aku nitori ẹṣẹ; ṣugbọn Ẹmmi awà li ayè nitori ododo.

11 Njẹ bi Ẹmmi ẹnniti o ji Kristi dide kuro ninọ oku ba wà ninọ nyin, ẹnniti ti o ji Kristi dide kuro ninọ oku yi o sì fi Ẹmmi rẹ̀ ti ọ wà ninọ nyin sọ ara oku nyin di ayè.

12 Njẹ ẹnyin ara, ajigbese li awa, ki iṣe ti ara, ti aofi wà nipa ti ara.

13 Nitori bi ẹnyin ba wà nipa ti ara, ẹnyin oku: ṣugbọn nipa ti Ẹmmi bi ẹnyin mba npọn ìṣe ti ara li oju, ẹnyi o yè.

14 Nitori iye awọn ti anṣe amọnna fu lati ọddọ Ẹmmi Ọlọrun wa, awọn ni iṣe ọmmọ Ọlọrun.

SI AWỌN ARA ROMU, VIII. 19

15 Nitori ẹnyin kò gba ẹmmi ideni lati bẹru mọ; ṣugbọn ẹnyin ti gba Ẹmmi isọdọmmọ, nipa eyi ti awa nfi nkepè, Abba, Babba.

16 Ẹmmi tikararẹ̀ li o njẹ ẹmmi wa li ẹri pe, ọmmọ Ọlọrun li awa iṣe.

17 Bi awa iba iṣe ọmmọ, njẹ awa li ajogun, ajogun ti Ọlọrun ati ajumọ jogun pẹllu Kristi; bi ọba ṣepe awa ba ajiya, ki a le iṣe wa li ogo pẹllu rẹ̀.

18 Nitori ti mo ti ṣirò rẹ̀ pe iyà igbà isisiyi kò yẹ lati fi ṣe akawe ogo ti aofihàn ninọ wa.

19 Nitori afojusọnna ireti ti ẹdda o duro de ifihàn awọn ọmmọ Ọlọrun.

20 Nitori ti ada ẹdda lati fi ori ballẹ fu assan, ki iṣe tinọtinọ rẹ̀, ṣugbọn nipa ẹnniti onfi ori rẹ̀ ballẹ ni ireti,

21 Nitori ti aọyọ ẹdda tikararẹ̀ kuro lọwọ idibajẹ si inọ idande ti oli ogo ti awọn ọmmọ Ọlọrun.

22 Nitori ti awa mọ pe gbogbo ẹdda li o nkerora ti o sì nrọbbi pọ titi ofi di isisiyi.

23 Ki isì iṣe awọn nikan, ati awa tikarawa pẹllu, ti o ni akọso Ẹmmi, ati awa tikarawa nkerora ninọ ara wa, awa nduro de isọdọmmọ, idande ti ara wa.

24 Nitori ipa ireti li afi ngba wa la: ṣugbọn ireti ti ari kì iṣe ireti: nitori ohun ti enia nri ki li o sì kun ti nreti fu.

25 Ṣugbọn bi awa mba nreti eyi ti awa kò ri, njẹ awa ama fi suuru duro de e.

26 Gẹggẹ Ẹmmi na pẹllu nran ailera wa lọwọ: nitori ti awa kò mọ ohun ti awa iba ma tọrọ bi

The eighth chapter of Romans in Yoruba, the language of south-west Nigeria. This translation first appeared in 1850.

one. He also knew that his remedy for escaping it had really worked in his own life. He had accepted the simple fact that Christ had suffered the death, the alienation from God, which was the result, not of his own wrongdoing, but of the wrongdoing of others. He had accepted the claims of the risen Christ on his life. He had been remade by the Holy Spirit's power. And as 'a man in Christ' he knew that he could always enjoy forgiveness and the dynamic power of a new life in his own experience: the risen life of Christ himself.

Equals before God

Paul also discovered that because of his new relationship with God, he could enjoy a new freedom in his relationships with other people. It simply made no difference whether they were men or women, Jews or Gentiles, slaves or masters, educated or ignorant. Paul came to see that all people are of equal value to God.

In this too Paul led the way for later generations, although Christians have often lost sight of the importance of this idea in his writings. Yet it is partly because of his insights that the evil of slavery was finally abolished in the western world – and in our own day the fight for racial and sexual equality owes much to the teaching of Paul, although few realize it.

Respecting others

Matthew 7:12

Because Paul felt that all men and women were of equal worth, he knew that he must always respect the feelings and beliefs of other people. His advice to the Christians at Corinth on the subject of eating idol-meat is a classic example of this. Jesus had taught that 'whatever you wish that men would do to you, do so to them'. Paul undoubtedly took this advice seriously.

In practice this sort of approach has often led to woolliness in applying Christian beliefs to everyday situations. But not so with Paul, a man with extremely strong convictions, who knew precisely what he ought to do and say. Today, strong beliefs often go hand-in-hand with intolerance, bigotry and narrow-mindedness. By contrast, Paul is the supreme example of how to be a man of firm conviction and an open mind.

It would be very difficult to find a single instance where Paul ever acused another Christian of being a 'heretic'. Only in the most extreme circumstances would he even consider the possibility of cutting off a Christian from the fellowship of the church. Although he disagreed violently with some of his opponents, he displayed a tolerance towards them that many after him would do well to copy. This above all is perhaps the most distinctive mark of a truly great man.

Yet the impression we get from the New Testament is that Paul would never have regarded himself as great. And it is certainly true that the real greatness of Paul lay not in his natural gifts, outstanding as these were; nor in his success as an able and adventurous missionary; nor even in his theological writings, although he wrote more than one third of our New Testament.

Paul is seen as a truly great man only when we view him as he saw himself: as 'a man in Christ'. He was a man who had denied himself in the most radical way possible, and for whom his risen Lord was everything:

> 'I count everything as loss
> because of the surpassing worth
> of knowing Christ Jesus my Lord.'

Philippians 3:8

Other Books on Paul

*Books marked * are recommended for more advanced study*

Chapter One Paul's Background

G. H. C. MacGregor and A. C. Purdy, *Jew and Greek: Tutors unto Christ*, Edinburgh, 1959, pp. 87–102, 239–258, 273–329. A very readable and helpful introduction to the political and religious background of the New Testament.

C. A. A. Scott, *Christianity according to St Paul*, Cambridge, 1927, pp. 1–16. This book also considers the possible relationship between Jesus and Paul.

*W. D. Davies, *Paul and Rabbinic Judaism*, London, 1970. A detailed comparison of Paul's theology with his background in Pharisaism.

*R. N. Longenecker, *Paul: Apostle of Liberty*, New York, 1964. Deals with the same subjects as W. D. Davies.

*J. G. Machen, *The Origin of Paul's Religion*, Grand Rapids, 1973 (repr.), pp. 211–317. Especially useful on Paul and the Mystery Religions.

*W. Schmithals, *Paul and the Gnostics*, Nashville/New York, 1972. An important study of Paul's opponents.

Chapter Two Paul's Conversion

F. F. Bruce, *The Book of the Acts*, London, 1954. See especially on Acts chapters 9, 22, 26.

The Chronology of Paul's Early Work

D. Guthrie, *New Testament Introduction*, London, 1970, pp. 458–465. Gives a simple survey of the various alternative views.

*W. M. Ramsay, *St Paul the Traveller and the Roman Citizen*, London, 1920 (14th edn). Expounds the view adopted in this book.

J. Knox, *Chapters in a Life of Paul*, Nashville/New York, 1950. Attempts to construct an understanding of Paul's life and letters independently of the book of Acts.

Chapter Three The Apostolic Council

F. F. Bruce, *The Book of the Acts*, pp. 298–324.

Galatians

*E. D. Burton, *A Critical and Exegetical Commentary on the Epistle to the Galatians*, Edinburgh, 1921. The best commentary on Galatians.

G. S. Duncan, *Galatians*, London, 1934. Easy to read, with a good account of the circumstances behind the letter as well as detailed comments.

D. Guthrie, *Galatians*, London, 1969. A verse-by-verse exposition of the letter.

Chapter Four Paul's Missionary Strategy

*J. Munck, *Paul and the Salvation of Mankind*, London, 1959.

1 and 2 Thessalonians

A. L. Moore, *1 and 2 Thessalonians*, London, 1969. Covers the main points of the letters without being too technical.

R. A. Ward, *Commentary on 1 and 2 Thessalonians*, Waco, 1973. A good commentary that also tries to show how the letters are relevant today.

*E. Best, *A Commentary on the first and second epistles to the Thessalonians*, London, 1972. Probably the best commentary on these letters, though not for the beginner.

Chapter Five 1 and 2 Corinthians

*K. Lake, *The Earlier Epistles of St. Paul*, London, 1911, pp. 120–175. An excellent account of Paul's dealings with the church at Corinth, and the various 'parties' there.

M. E. Thrall, *The First and Second Letters of Paul to the Corinthians*, Cambridge, 1965. An easy-to-understand book on Corinthians.

*C. K. Barrett, *A Commentary on the first epistle to the Corinthians*, London, 1968.

*C. K. Barrett, *A Commentary on the second epistle to the Corinthians*, London, 1973. Professor Barrett's two books are the best commentaries on 1 and 2 Corinthians, though they could be heavy going for the beginner.

Romans

F. F. Bruce, *Romans*, London, 1963.

*C. K. Barrett, *A Commentary on the epistle to the Romans*, London, 1962.

Chapter Seven Colossians and Philemon

R. P. Martin, *Colossians and Philemon*, London, 1974.

Ephesians

D. Guthrie, *New Testament Introduction*, London, 1970, pp. 479–521. Deals with questions of date and authorship, arguing that Paul wrote Ephesians.

W. G. Kümmel, *Introduction to the New Testament*, London, 1966, pp. 247–258. A different view of the authorship and origin of Ephesians.

F. F. Bruce, *The Epistle to the Ephesians*, London, 1961. A simple exposition of the letter.

Philippians

R. P. Martin, *Philippians*, London, 1959.

*R. P. Martin, *An Early Christian Confession*, London, 1960. An examination of the 'Christ hymn' in Philippians 2:5–8.

The Pastoral Epistles

*P. N. Harrison, *The Problem of the Pastoral Epistles*, London, 1921. Puts forward the view that they were composed out of scraps of Paul's letters.

C. K. Barrett, *The Pastoral Epistles*, Oxford, 1963. An excellent commentary, written on the basis of a view somewhat similar to Harrison's.

J. N. D. Kelly, *A Commentary on the Pastoral Epistles*, London, 1963. Argues for Paul's authorship.

Paul's Imprisonments

G. S. Duncan, *St Paul's Ephesian Ministry*, London, 1929. The book referred to in our discussion of the subject.

D. Guthrie, *New Testament Introduction*, London, 1970, pp. 472–478. Examines Duncan's theory.

Chapter Eight Paul's Theology

D. E. H. Whiteley, *The Theology of St Paul*, Oxford, 1964. A comprehensive analysis of Paul's thought. Beginners may find it a little demanding, but perseverance will be well rewarded.

G. Bornkamm, *Paul*, London, 1971. A full account of Paul's life and letters.

*R. Bultmann, *Theology of the New Testament*, I, London, 1952, pp. 187–352. Definitely not a book for the beginner, though most important for a complete understanding of Paul.

*J. W. Drane, *Paul: Libertine or Legalist?*, London, 1975. Investigates the relationship between Romans, Galatians and 1 and 2 Corinthians and deals with the identity of Paul's opponents in these letters. Provides more detailed arguments for some of the positions adopted in this book.

Index